An Ordinary Man

A Baby Boomer Biography
1952-1974

Peter D Canfield

ISBN-13: 9781521998984

TABLE OF CONTENTS

THE STORY BEGINS

I don't know why I believe it, but I do believe it to be a good idea to try to write an autobiography. Not because I am someone rich and famous, but because I am not famous or rich, or even notorious. I'm just an ordinary man.

There is an old Chinese curse that says, "May you live in interesting times!" I am a guy who lived in, and grew up in, interesting times - or, at least as much as I have grown up, I did so in an interesting time. That time, the 1960s and early 70s, with its turmoil, social and cultural revolution, evolution, explosions and implosions, made a substantial contribution in creating who I have been and who I have become. There are certainly times when I wish that influence had been less. I am, however, fairly content in my life, now. As this document is being created and written down, the year is 2016, it is early winter and I am 64 years old.

I guess if this is an autobiography, I ought to introduce myself, or at least tell you my name. I'm Pete. Specifically, my name is Peter Douglas Bartley Canfield. The rest of the book will be, or perhaps, should be, the introduction, if properly done.

It is pretty much a given that some of the stories will be out of chronological order, but I'm pretty sure that you will get the general idea. I will try not to confuse Kindergarten with Army basic training, although there are some similarities. Other than that, it is my intent to maintain some semblance of a straight time line. Just remember, the more recent the memories, the greater the chance that they may be in a somewhat straighter time line. They may even a bit more accurate.

I'm reasonably sure that I was born August 5, 1952. Things happened thereafter. I grew, I was educated, made friends, fell in love (more than once), fell out of love (also more than once), made good choices, and made some bad choices. All of these things combined to make me, me. Or, at least the "me" that I am now.

Again, they tell me that I was born on August 5, 1952. I don't actually remember it, of course, because I was very young at the time. My parents were William Norman Bartley and Wilma Nadine (Ward) Bartley. I remember very little of my first few years although there are a number of vague vignettes that course through my memories from time to time. Some I may actually remember. Others may be of family legend that grow and take on new meaning and character with each new telling, each new embellishment, and each new glance through old photo albums.

In another sense, some of what I remember may have, indeed, been remembered for me by other, older family members, and then "gifted" to me at a later time. Not every memory is remembered chronologically, and there are times when I simply cannot remember which event occurred in what order. Some folks' memories are so well developed, however, that they can even remember stuff that never even happened! And, different folks often do remember the same things and the same occasions, only they remember them... differently.

At a bare minimum, I will try to make sure that the event, whatever it may be, will at least be in the right locale and in the correct time frame for each locale. My early life happened sequentially, in one place after another, within just a few relatively close locales. We did, however, live in some of these locales more than once. We lived in Midway City, California, first in 2 different locations, one on Washington Ave, and one on Roosevelt Ave, and second, in different time frames, once before Rock Springs Wyoming, and once after Rock Springs.

We lived in the Roosevelt house in Midway City both before and after Rock Springs Wyoming. We lived in Wyoming twice, once in Rawlins, in 1956, and once in Rock Springs, from 1960 to 1964. OK, that should have sufficiently confused the issue for now.

As I said, I will try to keep the events in the correct location, and the locations in correct chronological order. As I contemplate the places I have called home, I now realize that I have lived in over 40 locations in a dozen states, from coast to coast and from border to border.

But, boy do I remember some of those events! It is my hope to share some part of my life with those who are inclined to wonder about where they came from, who they came from. I hope my children take the time to read it, and I hope my grandkids will read it. And I truly hope that several generations hence, some, one, or more, of my descendants will be curious enough to peruse my thoughts and memories.

Memories truly are something to share. I was born in the 1950s, grew to maturity in the 1960s and early 1970s, served in the US Army during the Viet Nam War, got married in the 1970s, had children and nurtured them into responsible adulthood in the 1980s and 1990s. I have lived in several different regions of the USA, and have found beauty and friendship everywhere I have been.

I worked in a packaging plant in Huntington Beach, California, served in the US Army from 1971 to 1976, made pizzas in an Italian deli, hung and taped drywall, done custom exhaust work, and worked in multiple convenience stores in multiple states. I mined clay in Colorado, and served in administrative law enforcement, operating highway truck scales in Colorado and Oregon.

I've worked in real estate and property management. I have been employed by State Tax Departments, as a Tax Service Representative in Washington and as a Revenue Officer in Washington State and in Las Vegas and Reno, Nevada. I ended my working career as a Medical Support Assistant at the VA Hospital in Loma Linda, California. While with the VA, I worked in Loma Linda twice, Las Vegas and Spokane.

There are probably some short-term jobs that I missed. Like the one day I spent stringing explosive grenades onto Prima-cord to drop down newly drilled oil wells. The grenades are designed to explode and perforate the well casing. This allows oil to flow into the pipe to be pumped out of the well. They didn't normally start drinking beer until after the morning beer delivery had been made, so I guess that was OK. Remember, rehab is for QUITERS!

Over the course of my life, I have made good decisions, and I have made bad decisions. I have very few regrets about the life I have lived. Even if I had the ability, there are very few changes I would make in my life. I am who I am because of the path I have travelled to arrive in the "here and now", and, truly, truly, "What a long, strange trip it has been."

My hope is to give some flavor of the times in which I have lived. It is not to be some dry history book, but my story, told as I remember it. With just a little luck, my life story may be a small window into the past. I hope you enjoy it!

And, just a caveat; I am not politically correct. The culture in the time of my childhood and youth was different from the culture of today. I can pretty much guarantee that some of the stories I tell herein have the potential to offend, and probably will.

Wilma Nadine Bartley and William Norman Bartley - circa 1948

William (Bill) N Bartley holding Peter Douglas Bartley - 1952

William N Bartley – Palestine 1947

THE EARLY YEARS

I remember the front of an apartment building, one in a series of pastel apartments, in a series of pastel quadrangles with grassy yards, young families and lots of children. It may have been in a place referred to in the family as "Carmellitas, California". (Note: The spelling is questionable. I have been unable to locate a city of this name, but it may have been the name of the apartment complex, itself.)

I remember playing with my brother, Darrell, and my sister, Celia. Darrell is 4 ½ years older than am I, and Celia, 2 years older than I. I think I rode a tricycle. I remember the beach. I remember walking, holding Mom's hand. I remember Mom in a wedding dress. I remember Darrell telling her that she was beautiful. I remember that she cried when he told her.

This may well be one of those memories from other family members. I am not sure if I remember it, or simply remember the telling of it at some time in the past, perhaps while watching one of Dad's 35mm slide shows. I remember the picture, but not sure if I remember the event.

I was three years old, I think, and the family lived in Rawlins, Wyoming. If I were three, then that would have been either 1955 or 1956. It could have been the summer that I turned four years old, 1956. Mom and Carl got married in August 1956, and Tony was born in August 1957, which makes me 5 years older than is he. I have to assume that Mom and Bill Bartley were divorced sometime before that. But I don't know. I am, at best, semi familiar with the sequence of events, but not so much with the actual time line.

I don't know the whole story, and it is probably no one else's business, but I have been told that Mom and Carl met at the Cowboy Bar in Long Beach, California. I'm pretty sure they were both of adequate age, and capable of enjoying a night out. Curiously, I don't remember Mom as being particularly fond of country music. She was more pop, swing and classical.

Carl Canfield was, and is, a professional man, a Petroleum Engineer. I have been told that Mom wasn't sure what a Petroleum Engineer was, but she did know what a Geologist was, so for a time, he was a geologist. He also was, and is, a farmer... and the best mechanic I have ever known... and a great gardener, and a carpenter, and a house painter, and, and, and! I just figured that if something was broken, Dad could, and would, just fix it, from cars to washing machines to television sets with vacuum tubes and a black and white picture.

Anyway, we were in Rawlins, Wyoming, and I was very young. There was Mom, Dad (Carl), Darrell, Celia and me. From this point forward, I will most often refer to Carl Canfield as "Dad", or "Pop", because he is the one who raised me and is the Father figure I remember.

Bill Bartley was a transitory figure when I was young, whom I just barely remembered. We tended to see him most often on birthdays and Christmas. I remember that he gave Darrell, Celia and me bicycles for Christmas, shortly before we moved to Rock Springs. That would have been 1959, I was 7 years old.

Our move to Wyoming effectively severed our connection with him. I don't think Mom and Dad made any effort to notify him when we returned to California.

He didn't reappear in our lives until Celia graduated high school. She looked for him, found him and invited him to her high school graduation.

Celia graduated when she was 18, so I must have been 16. In every sense, I met my father for the first time when I was 16 years old. Before that, all I had was the remains of a shadow of a memory.

Bill Bartley and I became good friends over time, but I had a Dad. Carl legally adopted me, gave me his name, raised me, and corrected me when I was wrong. He taught me how to change a tire and how to fish.

More importantly, he taught me how to man up when I screw up. He did a lot of teaching simply by the way he lived, the way he treated others, and the way others respected him and responded to him.

Bill Bartley and I did enjoy each other's company. In our respective military services, his in the Navy, and mine in the Army, we shared that bond of military service. I see in myself, the influence of both men, with parts of each contributing to create the man, the person, that I have become.

Again, we lived in Rawlins, Wyoming. I was young. I was very, very young.

There were workmen working on the street in front of our abode. I remember barricades and piles of dirt, the road torn up. I don't remember if we had a house, an apartment, a trailer, a tent, or a tipi, whatever. But, for a short period of time, we lived there.

As I watched them work through the summer, the guys on the crew took a liking to me. On occasion, they would buy a Popsicle for me from the corner Mom and Pop grocery store. I seem to think it was just for a summer, but don't seem to remember much more. End of that memory. I don't know why it's there, but it is.

Darrell, Celia, and Peter – Carmalitos, CA circa 1953/1954

Newlyweds Carl M and Wilma N Canfield – August 1956

\

MIDWAY CITY CALIFORNIA

I was a little older, or perhaps, just a little less young. We lived in Midway City, California, an unincorporated area in Orange County. We were just a few, short miles from Southern California beaches in a semi-rural area with a laid back, California sunshine, agricultural feel. Our neighborhood was surrounded by fields of vegetables, rows of corn, oranges groves and strawberry fields. Neighbors kept chickens, and we would hear the roosters' early morning crow, the hens clucking and bragging amongst themselves.

I remember the house. It is still there on Washington Street. It was, and still is, light yellow, stucco home with white trim, the last house before the "field". The "field" was a grass and weed filled power-line right-of-way, with lots of open space that seemed to go on forever. We didn't need a fancy public park; we had the "field"—more on the field, later.

It was early summer 1957 and Mom was pregnant with Tony. Mom and Dad had friends over to visit. They had, of course, brought their children, the same ages as Darrell and Celia. As the adults visited inside, Celia and Darrell were expected to entertain the visiting children outside and keep an eye on me. We played tag, chased each other around the yard, yelling, acting like kids in the warm summer twilight, Southern California 1957.

One of the kids found a coil of rope in the garage, and someone else decided it was a good idea to tie our parents' car to their parents' car, both of which were parked at the curb in front of the house. We loosely wrapped the rope between the bumpers, with multiple loops around each and then simply left the 2 cars tied together. We went back to running around in the evening.

Just after sunset, while still fairly light outside, the adults began saying their goodbyes; each began collecting their respective offspring. Mom, very pregnant with Tony, stood on the lawn with Dad waving goodbye.

Mom, unaware, was standing in a loop of the rope we had used to tie the cars together. When the car pulled away from the curb, it pulled Mom's feet out from under her! She fell hard on her back. The other car, reaching the end of the rope, jerked to a stop.

There was a lot of concern that Mom or perhaps even the unborn baby had been hurt. They both seemed to be OK, although I am pretty sure that Mom went to the doctor to be checked out. This might well be one of those memories, reinforced over the years by the retelling within the family. I think I remember the event, but I could be wrong. It may have been remembered for me by others in the family.

The folks were NOT happy, and we had absolutely no doubt that they were NOT happy. They told us why, and, in some detail, explained the laws of actions, reactions and consequences for actions. We were informed in clear, simple, unmistakable language that this had not been one of our brightest endeavors. And, believe me, the consequences of these actions left a definite imprint; primarily on our nether regions! I managed to avoid most of those physical consequences, because I was the youngest, and they were supposed to be keeping me out of mischief.

I really don't know why, but I remember having Jewish neighbors. The fact of their religion never had and, indeed, still doesn't have any bearing on who they were or their friendship with my family. I don't know why their religion would have any bearing on anything. This is just one small piece of information in my story.

The father's name was also Peter, which may be why I remember. They had a son named Nathan, I believe. I cannot remember the Mom's name. Our families were friendly, but with different traditions.

The two Dads would sometimes work in the garage on cars or lawn mowers or other things, as neighbors do. They would sometimes sit and visit with each other over a cold beer. I do remember that we had more similarities than we had differences. We understood Chanukah, and they understood Christmas. We knew that we were all from the same "root and branch" of Judeo-Christianity.

Also, the other neighbor's dog killed Darrell's guinea pig. The guinea pig had gotten out of the cage, and the dog chased it, caught it, and killed it. The funeral was appropriately solemn.

It was shortly thereafter that we moved a few blocks up to Roosevelt Street, still in Midway City. When asked, Pop told me that they got the house for $10,000. We had been living in it for some time, and the developer was very motivated to sell; they had been negotiating for some time now.

Mom and Dad didn't have the necessary down payment. The developer finally, mostly out of frustration, said that if they would just sign the contract, he would consider the next rent payment as the down payment. Thereafter, all they had to do was to make the mortgage payments. So that's what they did. That was in 1958.

Since then, that home has been enlarged with 2 new bedrooms and another bathroom added on. According to Zillow, although not on the market, it is currently, in 2017, valued at $695,000!

I'm not sure how long we lived in the house this time around. Tony was born in 1957, and we moved to Rock Springs in 1959 or '60, so it could only have been a couple of years.

This was a working class neighborhood, although, at that time, we were mostly unaware of class distinctions. We lived much as our neighbors did. We had a dog or two, mowed the lawn on weekends, had a vegetable garden in the back yard, a bamboo grove, and a cactus garden. Dad had planted fruit trees when we first moved in.

I remember the cactus garden quite well, thank you. I was running around the back yard, playing with our dog, Misty. She later produced a pair of pups whom we named Rocket and Missile. This was during the Cold War and the Race for Space, a time of strong American Patriotism. In so naming them, we were totally in sync with the times.

Anyway, Misty jumped up on me, and I fell backward into the cactus garden! With the dog on top of me! Terrible pain, as cactus spines poked and punctured me from one end to the other. Mom heard my yell, and came running out. She spent quite a while with the tweezers, gently pulling thorns from my hide. I did not enjoy this activity as a child, nor do I recommend it for other children. It HURT!

Our back yard had been the staging ground for the construction project that had built our entire neighborhood of modest, California tract homes. We kids scoured the yard for nails that Dad could use on other projects. He converted a leftover advertising signboard into a ping-pong table. He used other leftover material to build shelves in the garage.

I, with my brother and sister, attended Midway City Grammar School, three blocks from home. My folks went to PTA meetings, Cub Scout and Boy Scout meetings and potluck dinners at the school.

I used Dad's lawn mower to mow neighborhood lawns. This is where my spending money came from. I charged from $3 to $5 per lawn, depending on the amount of work required. Of course, to use Dad's mower, I had to first mow our lawn.

I had a steady clientele of between three and five neighbors for whom I would mow each week. At that time, $10 to $15 a week was a lot of money. Candy bars were a nickel, a bottle of Coke, Pepsi or Nehi soda, grape or orange, a dime. Going to the movie cost twenty cents, and popcorn, a dime.

A gallon of gas was twenty cents, and you got dishes or hand towels when you filled the tank!

We played in the neighbor's yards, and the neighborhood kids played in ours. It seemed that we were always outside, doing... something! Bikes, beaches, baseballs, basketballs, whatever. We seemed to be forever on the move, going somewhere, doing something.

Families did things together. Parents, mostly Moms because the Dads all worked, took us to the beach and other activities. And, if you were there when they said they were going to the beach, they always seemed to make room for one more kid. Or two, or three, or more kids. You just shoved them into the station wagon, and off we'd go.

We took day trips to the beach or to O'Neil Park in Trabuco Canyon, and participated in Cub Scouts and Brownies, Girl Scouts and Boy Scouts, PTA meetings and the occasional potluck dinner in the Midway City School Cafeteria. It seemed that everyone in the neighborhood was, in some way, involved in the neighborhood.

Dad was a Cub Scout and Boy Scout Parent/Leader and Mom was involved with Girl Scouts and Brownies. Mike and Tim's dad, Ed, was also involved in Scouting. When Parent/Teacher conferences were held, both parents attended. When the Scouts had a barbeque or picnic, everyone showed up. There were softball games, three legged races, wheelbarrow races and other events involving the entire family.

It was a good time in America, an innocent time. Yes, there was trouble in the world, but as kids, we were pretty oblivious to that trouble. I think that was, and is, a lucky thing. At that time, and in that world, we were allowed to be kids. Just, kids.

The weather in coastal Southern California was, for the most part, very temperate. In winter, the temps might drop into the 50s, and summers were usually in the 80s. It could, however, get well into the 100s. I have empirical data as to the truthfulness of that statement.

I have been reminded by various family members of a summer incident in which I stood barefoot on the metal manhole cover in the middle of our street. I was screaming and hopping from foot to foot, as the scorching hot manhole cover, heated by the Southern California summer sun, burned and blistered my tender feet. I wasn't yet smart enough to get out of the street, off the manhole cover and onto the grass. Dad finally figured out what the problem was, hurried out and carried me into the grassy yard. A valuable lesson learned. I won't be doing that again.

There was an occasion when the neighbor boys went up to Big Bear and brought back a truckload of snow. I call them neighbor boys, because although they had their driver's license, they were teenagers, not yet adults. They dumped the snow in the middle of the cul-de-sac. The neighborhood kids, some of whom had never seen snow, played happily in it until it melted.

We did manage to make the very best snowman within 5 miles of the beach, and probably should have gotten a ribbon for it. We didn't, of course, because back then you actually had to do something extra to get ribbons and awards. Admittedly, there was very little competition in this event.

Pete – Southern California Beach circa 1957

Carl and Nadine Canfield – Midway City, CA circa 1959

Celia and Pete Canfield being Kids – Midway City, CA circa 1958

Southern California snowman – circa 1959

ROCK SPRINGS, WYOMING

Sometime after First Grade, not being sure if Second Grade had started yet or not, our family moved from Southern California to Rock Springs, Wyoming. In a rather ironic twist, it didn't matter if Second Grade had started or not, because I got to do it twice! Wow. The nuns at Sts. Cyril and Methodius Catholic Grammar School actually flunked me.

I said I didn't care, I was going to Third Grade anyway. I was defiant! Catholic nuns were, at that time, a totally unknown phenomenon. I didn't win this battle, not by a long shot. Sister Mary John Ella was a force of nature, not to be trifled with. And, my parents agreed with HER!

On a cold and snowy winter day, I came home from school crying. When Mom asked why, I told her that Sister Mary John Ella had called me a DIRTY ELEPHANT! I was but 7 or 8 years old, and Mom was curious, so she called the school and spoke with Sister.

As she listened, I saw her smile but try not to laugh. She couldn't hold it in, and began laughing until tears streamed down her cheeks. I was sorely offended that my grievance was being taken so lightly. Later that evening, as she told the story to Dad, she concluded by saying Sister did not call me a DIRTY ELEPHANT, but said that I had been a disturbing element in the classroom!

The Parish Priest, Father Gnedovic, of Slavic descent, was from "the Old Country". Some of us could actually understand his English, despite his thick, Slavic accent, an accent even more pronounced when he celebrated Mass in Latin.

Father Sullivan, the assistant parish priest, was a young Irishman with a distinct brogue. He had a sparkle in his eye and was put in charge of the elementary school, boys' choir. We sang not only hymns, but we also sang Frankie Valli and the Four Seasons, "Walk Like A Man".

Regardless of what may have happened elsewhere, there were no allegations of impropriety here in Rock Springs. Both priests were good and Godly men. I learned a lot from both of them. Fr. Gnedovic has since gone to his reward, and I have lost track of Father Sullivan. As you can imagine, there are a lot of Father Sullivans. Finding the right one is simply not possible.

Anyway. Throughout most of grade school, I attended the Catholic Grade School of Sts. Cyril and Methodius, named for a pair of Slavic Saints of some medieval time frame. And this in Rock Springs, Wyoming, 1960, population 10,371.

Rock Springs, Wyoming was established by coal miners in the 1850s, providing coal for the Union Pacific railroad. They employed miners from all over the world, from the Slavic nations of Eastern Europe, from Sweden, Germany, France, England and China.

Bad blood developed between the miners from Europe and those from China. In 1885, a major labor riot erupted between the European and Chinese miners, resulting in the deaths 28 Chinese miners, with 15 more seriously injured.

This event became known as the Rock Springs Massacre. The US Army was eventually brought in to quell the violence. Although several were identified by credible witnesses, none of the European miners were ever charged with any crimes.

I don't recall being taught about that particular incident in the Rock Springs schools. That page in the history books had been, somehow, overlooked and omitted. I accidently stumbled upon the story much later in life while researching Rock Springs history. Rock Springs remains a major coal producer, and a regional center for energy exploration and production.

My schoolmates had Slavic names like Yakomovich, Kusic, Koritnik, and Pototchnik. The Parish school potluck dinners were wonderful, the smells of ethnic cooking permeating the neighborhoods.

The term "culture shock" had not yet been coined, but we would have been a prime example of just that; transplants from suburban Southern California to Wyoming's high desert. The one thing everyone wanted to know was if we had been to Disneyland. We were, after all, from California. And, that's where Disneyland is!

Yes, we had gone to Disneyland, although not often. The cost may not have been exorbitant, at least for the times, but the additional associated costs were not insignificant. Admission, rides, food, drinks and souvenirs could add up rather quickly.

We lived about five miles from Disneyland, and could see the nightly fireworks display from our backyard. However, it seemed that we only went to Disneyland when someone from out of town came for a visit.

We also went to Knott's Berry Farm. At that time there was no admission charge to Knott's, and Mr. and Mrs. Knott were occasionally seen at the Farm. The men visiting Knott's Berry Farm, for the most part, wore suits and ties, the ladies, dresses, hats and gloves. A proper Lady never went out without her gloves and a suitable bonnet.

The workers at Knott's wore coveralls and jeans or other Western wear. And gentlemen wore hats. They wore Fedoras, bowlers, straw-hats of various kinds, western hats and others. For that matter, Knott's Berry Farm had a pretty good hat shop as part of its Old West General Store. And, yes, we had been to the beach and had swum in the ocean. And no, I had never been eaten by a shark!

At Saints Cyril and Methodius School, Father Gnedevic, drove the school bus. His driving encouraged many of us to pray. It also taught us to sit down, shut up, and hold on for dear life. There was a serious, legitimate fear of someone being thrown down the bus aisle . . . again! Or, perhaps even being thrown out through the front window of the bus!

The only controls with which he appeared to be familiar, were the gas pedal and the horn. Although there were times we would rather have walked the several miles to school, I don't remember anyone actually being killed by Father's driving, but the potential was, without a doubt, still there.

In preparation for the move to Wyoming, my folks decided to sell one of the cars. They decided to sell the Chrysler, simply because the Chevrolet had better tires. The Chrysler was, overall, a better car than the Chevy. Dad would drive the Chevy from California to Rock Springs. The rest of us would take the train.

It's funny, how simple, every day decisions are made. It boiled down to which car had the better tires. Actually, that made it an easy decision. Get rid of the one with bald tires and keep the other one. Just so you know, I would seriously love to have either car, today.

Neither Mom's light green Chrysler nor Dad's dark blue 1948 Chevy sedan had automatic transmissions. They were both 3-speed transmissions, with the shifting lever on the steering column, known as a "3 on the tree".

My brother, Tony, of the rope footed Mom, although born in 1957, thought for the longest time that he had been born on the train. That train trip from Southern California to Rock Springs, Wyoming was one of his first complete memories.

It wasn't until he was a teenager that this issue came up, and, after laughing with him, and at him, we convinced him that it was simply not so. He had been born in a hospital in California, the same as the rest of us.

The name on his birth certificate is Carlton Dana Canfield. However, because he looked so much like the neighborhood, Italian bread man, his name in the family has always been Tony.

In Wyoming, there were no beaches. Or at least, there were no ocean beaches. There were, however, other activities that, conversely, were not available in Southern California.

Things such as ice skating, where you strapped sharpened blades on your feet and learned to propel yourself forward across some iced over body of water. And, after several spills and collisions with rocks, weeds, tree stumps and other ice-skaters, as well as certain amount of blood spilled, you also learned to stop.

Perhaps most importantly, we learned how to determine if the ice was thick enough to skate on. If we walked out on the ice, broke through and fell into freezing water, then the ice was not thick enough for skating. We also learned that the best way to test the ice was to get some other kid to walk out on the ice and see if that kid fell through the ice!

We would begin our ice testing in late fall by throwing rocks out on the ice. We would incrementally increase the test weight, contingent upon being able to talking some small, skinny kid into walking out on the ice. If he didn't fall through, we would work our way up through bigger and heavier kids until we got to that fat kid that lived in the last trailer in the far corner. If he didn't fall through, we were all good! Let's go skating!

We spent most of our time in our back yard, several hundred thousand square miles of high desert: sagebrush, cactus, lizards, horned toads, jackrabbits, rattlesnakes, bull snakes, sidewinders and garden snakes of various kinds, coyotes, bob cats, sheep and sheep-herders with their shepherd dogs.

There were, and probably still are, a seemingly unlimited number of dirt roads that crisscross the high desert in southwestern Wyoming. I don't think anyone knows where they all go, assuming that they actually go anywhere. When you follow some of them, you will come across old, abandoned dugout shelters, used by pioneers in the great western expansion after the Civil War. There are old wagon trails with the wheel ruts still visible, old powder lockers dug into the hillsides, used by the first miners in the region.

There are canyons and ravines that seasonal rains and flash floods have worn deep into the earth. In some places, you might not be able to climb out for several miles. We kids, though, knew many of the paths and dirt roads, and used them for our own adventures. We had unbelievable freedom! It was a wonderful, exciting time and place to be a kid!

Darrell had a paper route delivering the Rock Springs Daily Rocket and Sunday Missile newspaper. It was a fairly large route, so I was recruited to help.

We were up at 4:30 am when the papers arrived. We folded them, rubber banded them, and in the winter, put them in the back of the station wagon. Dad drove the route and Darrell and I rode on the tailgate, throwing papers in the general direction of the houses.

Some houses had designated receptacles for the paper. We would have to walk up and put them in that box. In the summer, Darrell loaded the news bags on his bike with papers and delivered most of the route. I delivered those in the trailer parks close to the house.

About a half mile across the highway was Killpecker Creek, where we would build rafts and catch pollywogs. We often played Army or Cowboys and Indians. We must have killed hundreds, if not thousands of enemy combatants. We built forts in clumps of sagebrush and in and around rock outcroppings. We were good! We could crawl from one hidden fort to another without being seen.

Part of the time we were dangerous, hostile Indians, creeping up on unsuspecting cowboy campfires, or on pioneer settlers on isolated homesteads. Other times, we were those cowboys and pioneer settlers. And often, we were heroic soldiers defending freedom from evil villains and Communist invaders.

From my current perspective, it seems that, as kids, that we had a lot of freedom. It was not unusual for boys as young as 12 or 13 years old to go hunting, usually with .22 cal rifles. Most often, the hunt was for jackrabbits, because the Hide and Fur Company bought them for $2.75 apiece. Darrell was given his .22 rifle for his 13th birthday.

The Sheepherders Association paid a bounty of $25 for coyotes and as much as $50 for bobcats and cougars. This is when my Dad, a petroleum engineer, was making around $750 to $800 per month. This kind of hunting could provide a steady, viable source of income.

We would hike the five miles or so to White Mountain. There was a spring where we would camp, fish and hunt. There was a window in late fall when it was cold enough for the rabbits to produce a good pelt, but still warm enough so we could camp for several days without freezing.

One of the neighbor kids found a book at the library with instructions on how to construct and use a sling to hunt. Not a sling shot, powered with rubber bands, but a biblical sling such as David used to slay Goliath. We discovered a specific technique to using it. It's not a matter of just swinging a rock around your head and letting go at random. With practice, you can achieve some degree of accuracy.

The railroad tracks were about a half-mile past Killpecker Creek. This line of the railroad carried ore cars from the lead mines farther north, up in Montana. For transportation, shipping and processing purposes, the ore was formed into balls roughly the size of a large marble. It made excellent ammunition for our slings!

We spent many hours in practice, and some of us became fairly adept. I'm not sure that we ever actually ever got a rabbit, but we certainly, completely, totally believed that we could, if we really wanted to!

Fireworks were legal in Wyoming for the week leading up to 4th of July. 100 firecrackers were $.25. Cherry Bombs were either a dime or a quarter each, as I remember. I think you could get 25 bottle rockets for a dollar. It was easy to use up several dollars worth in a really good bottle rocket war!

Everyone had their favorite small piece of ½ inch plumbing pipe to use as a launcher. Some had handles attached, some were just a length of pipe. We would aim them at each other and fire them off. If you saw the other fellow lighting it, you could usually dodge it.

For a really good bottle rocket war, we waited until after sunset. In the dark, the effect was so much better; bottle rockets crisscrossing, firecrackers and cherry bombs exploding! What kid could ask for anything more?

I didn't say it was safe or smart, but at that time, and in that place, it was something we did, and damn it, it was fun, even if it was foolish. All the fireworks did was to add, for a short time every summer, a small dose of special effects sight, sound and realism to our games. A few people got minor burns every year. I guess we were very fortunate that no one got seriously hurt.

We played "Army" all over the sagebrush-covered hills, through washes, arroyos, canyons and dry creek beds. We built paths and fortresses amongst the rocks and sagebrush. Some of the forts had hidden paths to and from other forts.

The kids, of course, knew the backcountry much better that did any of the adults. When we took off, more often than not we would just indicate to our parents a rather general direction of travel.

We lived in an area north of town. Most of our neighbors were employed in the blue-collar industries of either the oil fields or coal mining, the two primary sources of employment for that Rocky Mountain Region. The kids were kind of a rough bunch, with fistfights, perhaps not common, but also, not rare. Our house was a standard, site-built house, mostly surrounded by a trailer park, with another, larger trailer park just across the highway.

Dad put up a picketed snow fence around the front yard. We dug post holes by hand with a post-hole digger, set the fence posts, then stretched the fence by tying it to the back of his 1948 Chevy, pulling it taut and nailing it to the fence posts.

We installed a lawn and built concrete steps. We laid a 50-gallon barrel on its side in the concrete steps for use as a doghouse. It seems we always had a dog.

Dad contracted with the Sherriff's mounted posse to clean out their horse stables. He would use the horse manure as fertilizer for our lawn and vegetable garden. This was a good deal for both parties. One man's s**t is another man's fertilizer.

For a short time, we had a marvelous mountain of magnificent manure in our front yard. It must have been all of 8 feet tall, and a good 15 feet around.

Of course, every kid in the neighborhood came over to play in it and on it, either as new ground for Tonka Truck construction, or just as a place to play King of the Hill. Regardless, Dad was not the local mom's most popular resident when their kids went home reeking of horse manure.

Every kid in the neighborhood had several Tonka trucks and other Tonka construction equipment. We built roads and bridges up and down the small canyon just above the house.

Some of our roads stretched nearly a mile long, winding along the contours of the barren, high desert canyons that we played in. We built bridges of scrap lumber across smaller arroyo feeding into the small canyon where we played.

To clear ground for the garden, Pop built a rocker out of scrap lumber with a coarse screen that we used to sift gravel and debris from the yard where he wanted the garden and the lawn. He paid us, though. We got 10 cents for each wagonload of gravel that we hauled out of the yard and a little more for the bigger rocks

It didn't take long to clear out the rock and gravel, till in the manure and plant a garden. That garden was something of an anomaly in the high desert country of Southwest Wyoming. People driving through towards Yellowstone Park would pull off the highway just to look at the garden.

When there was excess produce, I was allowed to sell some of the produce in a roadside stand as my reward for helping in the garden. Many of my vegetable customers were travelers on Highway 187 North who stayed overnight in the trailer park.

There was fishing at 14 Mile Reservoir, a stocked pond, strangely enough, about 14 miles north of town. About 100 miles north of Rock Springs was Big Sandy Reservoir, and 30 miles north of Big Sandy was Pinedale Wyoming, with access to Fremont Lake, Half Moon Lake, Willow Lake and at least a half dozen others, all good fishing lakes.

About half way between Rock Springs and Pinedale was the small, picturesque Church at Farson, built of native rock and stone. It had been built by Father Gnedevic and volunteers from Rock Springs. Parish fishermen stopped at Farson for the Sunday 5:00 o'clock Mass on their way back to Rock Springs.

I can't remember if the little Church even had a name. Father drove the 40 miles or so every Sunday afternoon during fishing season. He was happy to do whatever it took to take care of his flock. He also liked to fish.

Mass was something that many looked forward to, so it was not out of the ordinary for the little chapel to be filled for the Sunday evening service. The parish folks were there, even if they did smell like fish. I'm sure it's OK, though. Most of the Apostles were fishermen.

Dad would also take us fishing in Green River, a town about 15 miles west of Rock Springs on Highway 30. This was also where to go to pick wild currants when in season. They do make the very best jams and preserves, although you were likely to be eaten alive by mosquitoes while picking them. For whatever reason, mosquitoes never bothered Dad. He just didn't seem to notice them.

We had a turquoise, 1960 Chevy Station Wagon, a true land yacht, some 17 feet long. It wasn't really our car, but a company car that Dad had free use of. We thought of it as ours, and several years later, when the company's fleet lease ran out, Dad did buy it.

It was something we needed. Mom, Dad, Darrell, Celia, Peter and Tony made for a pretty full load. There was room in the back for the fishing gear, picnic supplies and the other essentials for a road trip with four kids. There were no child car seats, and although the car may have had seat belts, I really don't remember them. We either sat in the seats, or rolled around in blankets in the back cargo area.

I do remember one camping trip in particular. We had driven to Fremont Lake, where we intended to camp for the weekend. Dad had walked around the shoreline for a bit of fishing, the kids were playing on the shore, and Mom was at the campsite.

Mom wanted a cup of coffee, but she could not get the camp stove to operate. It was a Coleman stove, operated on white gas. To operate, it had to be pressurized with a hand pump and lit with a match. Mom simply could not make it work.

By the time Dad returned to the campsite with several freshly caught fish, Mom had packed everything up. The car was loaded and Mom was ready to return to civilization. She really wanted a cup of coffee.

On another fishing trip, Dad and some of his friends had found, built, bought, brought, stolen or in some other manner came into possession of a homemade raft. While fishing from the raft, one of them saw a fishing rod and reel on the bottom of the lake. As I recall, it was only about 50 feet from shore, and some 20 or so feet deep, the water, crystal clear. The men decided they needed to rescue it.

As the wives on shore made jokes about Tom Sawyer, Huck Finn and men that don't grow up, the men tried several times to hook the pole with a fishing lure and bring it to the surface, which they eventually accomplished. I think Dad still has it. The evening's campfire had a lot of good-natured "I told you so's", from both the wives and the husbands.

Somewhere between fishing trips and gardening, Mom got pregnant again. This time, with Patricia. Mom thought to name her Jenny, but Dad protested, saying, "A Jenny's a mule!" Patty was born in April, just 3 days after Mom's birthday. Mom lamented, "If she had been born 4 days sooner, I would have been a year younger!"

While in Rock Springs, I joined, first Cub Scouts, and then promoted to Boy Scouts. About once a month in the spring and summer, our Boy Scout troop would gather together for an overnight campout. The boys would gather at the church and hike out of town under the direction and supervision of the older Scouts.

We usually had some direction in mind, but not always a destination. It was never about a goal to reach, but an event to experience. I do remember specifically one camping trip to an Aspen grove. We hiked a couple miles out of town, I believe to the Northeast.

Although Sweetwater County Wyoming is semi-arid high desert, there are occasional streams, creeks and isolated groves of various types of trees. As I recall, this Aspen grove in which we camped was all one tree, sharing the same root system, covering what must have been a couple of acres.

Before leaving our homes for overnight camping events, we prepared our dinners. These dinners consisted of shredded potatoes and carrots mixed together with seasoned hamburger, wrapped in tin foil and thrown into the campfire coals to cook.

More often than not, it ended up being some variation of steak tartar. It was always pretty raw, no matter how long we left it in the coals, but I'm pretty sure it didn't kill me. Most teenage boys have a cast iron stomach, anyway. They will eat things a sensible adult would throw away. And they enjoy it!

Boy Scout Summer Camp was for a week or so at the Scout Camp at Fremont Lake, near Pinedale. There was camping, canoeing, fishing, the making of leather wallets and moccasins, archery, and rifle marksmanship. We had to write a letter home to our parents. Might have even have had to write two letters and send them both.

My brother, Darrell, was too old for St Cyril & Methodius Catholic School. So he attended Rock Springs Public Junior High and then Rock Springs High School while we were there. Celia attended Sts C&M for a couple years, then matriculated to Rock Springs Junior High.

As I said earlier, Dad was a Petroleum Engineer. Because he was a Field Engineer, as opposed to an Office Engineer, he spent substantial time in the Wyoming oil fields, from Rock Springs to Rawlins, into the Wind River Mountains, and beyond. I would sometimes accompany him on these excursions. On several occasions, we got snowed in or stranded on the side of the highway, due to severe storms, including blizzards, even in the summer months!

Dad kept a box of emergency food and supplies, as well as sleeping bags, blankets and pillows in the back of the station wagon. For a long time, the very idea of Vienna sausages with hard tack and canned peaches was more than I could bear.

In that 1960 station wagon, with the back seats folded down we would stretch out in our sleeping bags and just wait it out. If the skip was right, we could even pick up distant radio stations, but only after dark when the stations could increase their power. We often listened to Oklahoma City and Kansas City stations out there in the middle of nowhere.

Where we were, out in the oil fields, there was a whole lot of nothing but miles and miles of nothing but sagebrush, coyotes, lizards, horny toads, snakes, badgers and other assorted critters. On our drives to and through the oil fields, we would see jackrabbits, American pronghorn and sage hens.

I was only 10 or 11 years old, but I got to know the roustabouts, drillers and others in the oil field, and they got to know me. It seems that I talked a lot and asked a million or so questions. As a consequence, in the oil fields, I was known as "Breezy", that kid that talks a lot.

In a sense, these rough men in a dangerous occupation adopted me, claimed me as one of their own. It felt good when we would pull up to a drilling rig and be greeted with calls of "Hi, Carl. Hey, Breezy!"

On one trip to the oil fields, the roustabouts discovered a badger digging a new burrow, and decided they should kill it. Several men got their guns from vehicles and started shooting the badger. It was a tough little critter, and it took a lot to kill it. At one point, the badger was trying to bite the barrel of the gun as it was being fired. I felt a little sick and didn't want to watch, but was somehow fascinated by the whole event. It took the better part of ½ hour to finally kill the poor beast.

Someone suggested that I should skin it and keep the pelt as a souvenir. I was given a hunting knife and very rudimentary instruction on how to proceed and sent downwind from the drilling site. Badgers can be VERY aromatic. This was not something that I had done before, nor did I really want to do it now.

I gritted my teeth and began the process. It was something I really didn't particularly want to do, but to "prove" myself, my masculinity, my manhood, to the oil field hands it was something that I had to do.

These men who had welcomed me into their hard world of strong, capable men had expectations of those in their ranks. These were hunters and fishermen, and squeamishness was not allowed. I was experiencing one of my "rites of passage", although I could have told you none of this at the time.

It took the better part of several hours to complete the task, but I finally had it done. I had removed the skin, but it was obvious that if I were left on my own, I would starve, as I had completely destroyed every part of the animal that might have been edible.

I was instructed to bury the carcass, and roll up the skin. I was to take it out every day and scrape off the excess meat, so I could get it down to just skin. They told me that the Indian women worked it by chewing it. Good for them, I thought. I sure ain't gonna do THAT!

I worked on it for the remainder of the week we were there, rolled it up and took it home. By the time we got home, it was beginning to reek, and had become infested with maggots.

There was no way on heaven or earth that Mom was going to allow this within 1000 yards of the house. Dad judiciously disposed of the pelt, but allowed me to keep the badger's tail. I know what happened to the pelt, but I have no idea what happened to the tail. Although in some macabre way, I wish I still had the tail, I was not really sorry to see the skin go. Again, it was not something I had wanted to do in the first place.

The night skies of Wyoming's high plains were often lit by massive, roaring fires as natural gas was burned off. Natural gas was a nuisance. They were after the oil, and there was no practical way to get the natural gas from the field to those civilized places where it might be put to use. The infrastructure did not yet exist. Nor, I might add, did today's environmental awareness.

It is incredibly difficult to explain a world to someone who did not experience it. The entire culture of American society was different. This was a time when most Americans were unaware that a nation called Viet Nam even existed. There were fewer still who could find it on a map.

In most families, the men worked at a job, and the mothers worked at home, raising kids, and maintaining the household. There were not a lot of two income families. But, at that time, one income was sufficient.

The world that I was raised in was very middle class. We were not wealthy, but we were also not poor. From before the time that I was five years old, my parents have owned every house that we lived in. We ate well, and we were dressed appropriately. The bills were paid, and there was often a little left over for recreation.

Most of the women who did work, worked as teachers, secretaries and nurses. There were few other fields open to them, although there were, and are, exceptions. Woman teachers were always either fairly young, or middle aged. The cycle seemed to be that, as soon as they married, their new job became "housewife", an honorable but underappreciated field. After their own children were sufficiently raised, they would return to the classroom and resume teaching.

Women were expected to be feminine at all times, and all men should be a mix of Robert Mitchum, James Coburn and Peter O'Toole, with a little Cary Grant and Sean Connery thrown in for class and style. The point being, men were strong, self sufficient and stylish. They could fight off sinister scoundrels, rebuild an engine, field dress a deer, and dress themselves with style and grace. They wished to be seen as sophisticated, manly men.

I would sometimes take Dad's .22 and hunt rabbits. I don't recall ever actually killing one, but I did shoot up a lot of ammunition. After watching Westerns on TV and in the movie theatre, I was more inclined to be hunting rustlers, outlaws and renegades, as opposed to rabbits.

On one occasion, Dad and I were out in the Wind River Mountains, near Elk Mountain, Wyoming, working on a well. The oil industry was a close-knit group, and they all knew one other. One of the other on-site engineers had membership in a nearby, private hunting lodge. He had keys to the gate and the lodge, and invited us to stay overnight. I was around 11 years old. As I recall, there were about a half-dozen men staying there, all associated with the oil industry; engineers, geologists, and technical specialists.

We sat up that night playing penny ante poker, and I was allowed to play along. It was only a penny to play, and I had some 60 cents to play with. We played 7-card stud, 5-card draw, and Spit in the Ocean. Boy, didn't I think I was something! Playing poker with the men!

In the morning, Dad pulled out his fishing pole and we went down to the private pond to try our luck. Sure enough, he pulled out a nice sized rainbow trout. She was very pregnant, so we had fresh trout and caviar for breakfast, along with our eggs and toast. We spent another couple nights sleeping in the lodge before returning to Rock Springs.

It was also in Wyoming that I began smoking cigarettes. I remember our neighbors, Scott and Jerry, Scott my age and Jerry, just a bit older, teasing me and blowing smoke in my face, trying to get me to smoke with them. I was 11 years old when I began smoking. I slowly became addicted to tobacco and was unable to break the addiction and quit tobacco until I was 61 years old.

I truly believe that this is the single thing I would change if I had it all to do over again. I would have walked away and never given in to the pressure to smoke. A major regret, now that I have a much better idea of what damage I have done by smoking. If you have to have a bad habit, pick something else.

At that time, smoking had much less social stigma than it has today. Actors smoked in the movies, and a gentleman always lit a lady's cigarette. Cigarettes and other tobacco products were advertised on television, on the radio, and in print. Medical reports concerning the hazards of smoking were just coming out at that time, which would have been in or around 1962 or 1963. Several cigarette commercials had medical doctors, MDs, promoting specific brands, because they were "safer" cigarettes!

There were charcoal filters, "micronite" filters and more. No one had ever heard of a "light" cigarette, and filtered and non-filtered were smoked just about equally. As I recall, ladies for the most part smoked filtered cigarettes, and men, "bare butt", non-filtered smokes.

When not camping or fishing or running around the hills, I was a Catholic Altar Boy. I took the requisite classes to learn the Mass in Latin, and served at the 40 Hour Devotional to The Virgin Mary in May.

Church was a significant part of our lives, with attendance at Mass every Sunday. The church and school were a single entity where we were taught to read and write, to add and to subtract. We also learned the teachings of the Catholic Church from the Baltimore Catechism, as taught by the Priests and the Nuns. Those not baptized as infants, were now baptized. We had our First Confession, our First Communion and our Confirmations of Faith. It was . . . . you know, normal!

The quality of education at Catholic school has been, in my experience uniformly superior. The equal application of reward and punishment created a positive learning environment. And, they'd smack you if you didn't learn right it the first time! Sorry, bad joke. In my opinion, I learned more in the Catholic schools I attended than I believe I would have in public schools.

I learned to drive in Wyoming. In addition to his 1948 Chevy Sedan, Dad had the company car, that 1960 Chevy Station Wagon. It was truly a land yacht, over 17 feet long!

As I said, I spent considerable time with Dad out in the oil patch. While out on dirt roads with nothing to run into, he taught me how to drive. I had to have a pillow behind me to reach the pedals, but I learned.

When Pop said I was a pretty good "seat of the pants" driver, he meant that I seemed to have a knack for it; I didn't jerk or stall out the engine. By the time I was 11 ½ or 12, I was actually a pretty good driver.

Wyoming in '60 through '64 was a great place to be a kid! We could hike for miles, our parents with nothing worry about except the possibility of chance encounters with coyotes, mountain lions, snakes and other critters. We could fall into a ditch and break a leg, or wreck a bicycle miles from home. We could be accidentally shot by sheepherders shooting at coyotes or other varmints.

There was no concern about too much television, as that was extremely limited. We only got 3 channels, ABC, NBC, and CBS, and they only broadcast from 6:00 in the morning until midnight when all three stations signed off with the Star Spangled Banner.

Television, for the most part, was pretty tame by today's standards. We enjoyed the music on the Lawrence Welk Show and the variety acts on The Ed Sullivan Show. We sang along with Mitch Miller and cheered as Roy Rogers roped bad guys and turned them over to the Sheriff. We enjoyed

Sea Hunt with Lloyd Bridges and The Wonderful World of Disney. We laughed at the Flintstones and got spooked with the Twilight Zone.

Computers, cell phones and other personal electronic devices had not yet been invented. The only place to find computers was in black and white, mad scientist movies, of which there were many. We thought it so very cool when Dad got a radiotelephone in the car, so Secret Agent Man! When out in the field, he would have to drive to the highest spot around just to connect with the mobile operator. You couldn't dial direct; you had to call the mobile operator to make a call.

Several other boys, and maybe a couple of girls, were out playing some version of 'follow the leader' in the rugged scrub that made up our play area. We were hiking up a path that ran diagonally up the steep face of a hill about 25 to 30 feet high. The path had a couple switchbacks, and someone above me dislodged a large rock, roughly twice the size of a basketball. With my standard luck, the rock struck me straight on in the groin! I was knocked down the hill, and landed, dusted and bloody, at the base.

My older brother, Darrell, and another kid carried me back to the house, as I was in no condition to walk. Mom rushed me to the hospital. Other than spending several hours curled up in the fetal position, no lasting damage was done... except, of course, for my pride. This was not a story I thought the neighborhood kids would ever let die. This was just one of the many benefits of growing up in a blue-collar world. If you showed a weakness, that just gave them something to aim at. Thankfully, someone else's story of misfortune would eventually replace mine.

It seemed that someone was always getting banged up. We had been sledding when Tony slid into my back and broke my ribs. He later ended up breaking his arm. This was a greater benefit than not, as it was discovered that he had a bone cyst, a part of his upper arm was essentially hollow. He underwent surgery in which the doctors attempted to take bone off of his hip and transplant it to his arm, but that attempt was not successful. They then tried unborn calf bone, and that worked. My brother, Tony, is now part cow. We like to ask him if he is bull, steer or heifer. How now, Brown cow?

We were out as a family to celebrate some family event, possibly a promotion for Dad. We were in one of Rock Springs nicer restaurants. It may not have been the nicest, but it was still a nice restaurant for our family, and for that time.

We were ready to enjoy a family meal, an opportunity to use and to display the table manners and civility that we had been taught. Dad was wearing a suit, Mom and Celia in dresses, and Darrell and I in our nicest jeans and button down shirts. Tony, all of two or three years old, had been fussing since before we left the house, and it seemed that nothing was going appease him.

He was in a high chair, and pushed up against the table. He kept reaching for things on the table, and would cry when he was not allowed to grab them. The meal came, and Tony was not settling down. He was, if fact, getting worse.

He reached for the table once again and nearly succeeded in spilling a plate full of food on the floor. When Mom pulled the plate back, he began screaming, disrupting the entire restaurant. Our quiet celebration was not going as planned. Dad had a glass half full of cold water in his hand, and, by instinct more than anything else, threw the icy water into Tony's face! There was instant silence! That tantrum was over!

I think everyone was shocked. Tony, with a face-full of ice water, certainly was. He had the most astonished look on his face I have ever seen, but most assuredly, was no longer screaming. Dad, having thrown that ice water had, I think, surprised himself, and Mom was astounded that Dad would have done so. Darrell, Celia and I were stunned, as were the other restaurant patrons and wait staff who had seen and heard what had happened. The entire restaurant was silent for a just few moments before returning to normal. I know that the remainder of that meal was one of the quietest, most civil, and best mannered ever for this family! We were all on our very best behavior.

My youngest sister, Patricia, born in April of 1962 developed epilepsy at a fairly young age. Mom tried to tell Dad about her symptoms, but he simply did not, and could not, understand, and brushed them off as "female hysteria"; until the first time he witnessed one of her grand mal seizures. He put Patricia in the car and drove her to the hospital.

He ran a red light and was speeding when he passed a police car going the opposite direction. The police turned their car around and began pursuit. Dad was driving so fast that they didn't catch up with him until he was at the hospital and on his way into the emergency room. Once they understood the situation, they chose not to pursue charges for reckless driving, speeding and running the red light.

Doctors tried a number of therapies, including sedatives such as Phenobarbital, which seemed to help control it. At some point in her teens, she simply outgrew it, and that was none too soon. It had been hard on the entire family, and there have been familial repercussions ever since.

My childhood in Wyoming has taken on an almost mythic stature in my memory. It was after all, a very long time ago in my life span, over 50 years ago. Small things, like sledding in the winter, running around the high desert, and the smell of burning coal are memories that occasionally jump to the forefront. A sound, a smell, a pattern, a street that looks familiar, these are all things that can bring it back. The stories neither invited nor rejected, just remembered.

I remember the basement, where my dad did stuff, and built stuff, and fixed stuff. I remember the old Halifax tube radio, listening to a country/western music radio station from Oklahoma City. Dad said it had something to do with "atmospheric skip". I remember watching "Sing Along With Mitch", "The Ed Sullivan Show", and "The Flintstones". Just as a point of interest, The Flintstones were the first married couple ever shown on television in the same bed. It was nearly scandalous!

There was a coal stove in the basement that kept the whole house warm. There is something about the smell of burning coal that you never forget. I know there are environmental issues at hand, but it was of much less concern then, and I choose not to monitor my memories, or suppress them now, because they might be frowned upon by today's standards. It was a different time, and different standards applied.

The Federal government, in the creation of Flaming Gorge Reservoir, decided to clean out the Green River of "undesirable" fish. They used rotenone, a poison that only kills some fish, those with scales. The plan was to re-stock the river with game fish. I vividly recall going to Green River to catch what we could of the poisoned fish.

Darrell caught hold of a massive carp, nearly as big as he was. He wrestled with it for a long time before finally dragging it to the shore. It may have been weakened, but it was still very much alive. There were people all up and down the river's banks, all of whom had come for the fish. There was no license required if caught by hand without the use any fishing gear except nets.

The poison works by taking oxygen out of the water, causing the fish suffocate. Although the poison killed the fish, there was nothing wrong with the meat of the fish. Many people saw it as free food. Obviously, this is not something that would be allowed today by the Federal Environmental Protection Agency, but it was all part of the much larger plan creating Flaming Gorge Reservoir.

Dad likes music. He can listen to swing, Dixieland and big band, but he likes country music. And he did NOT like Rock n' Roll. Darrell did, Celia was starting to, and Mom liked some of it. I remember her singing "The Wayward Wind", by Gogi Grant. I remember her standing at the foot of my upper bunk bed, singing "I ain't got nobody . . . " from Louis Prima's song, "Just a Gigolo", rolling her head back and forth, as though she had no body.

OK, not exactly Rock 'n Roll, but it sure wasn't country. OK, maybe you had to be there, but I was only 7 years, and to me, it was funny. I seem to remember that everybody liked the folk music that was becoming more popular over the radio. Pete Seeger, Peter, Paul and Mary, Bob Dillon, and the Kingston Trio were all on the charts in 1962.

There was a hill just north of our home, a rock formation that the kids called Gorilla Rock. They probably still call it Gorilla Rock. It was a small hollow on top of the hill surrounded by boulders...with firing ports for musket and cannon, and another rock perched on the high side of the hollow, obviously the lookout's post.

At various times this small hilltop fort had been everything from a Knight's Castle to a Cavalry Outpost to a Pirate's Ship. It had been occupied by both friend and foe--both attacked and defended.

We were several, the children of the oil field worker's trailer park. There was the Sullivan family, a good Catholic family with 9 kids in a 3-bedroom trailer, and the Jehovah Witness family in the other site-built house, two boys and a girl. The boys were Scott and Jerry, and they are the ones that got me started smoking cigarettes. Scott was my age, and Jerry just a bit older than we were by perhaps up to three years. I was 11 years old.

Scott and I, when not being friends, would beat the snot out of each other. We always seemed to find something to fight about. At some times, it would be religion, at other times the best TV program, at other times about whether his sister liked my brother, or his brother liked my sister. It really did not matter. Eventually, we would always find something to fight about. I guess it was actually pretty good training for both of us. As least we didn't just lie down and cry when someone hit us. We learned to hit back.

That may not be politically correct now, but it worked for us, and for a lot of the other kids in our blue-collar enclave. We took care of our own business. Kids fought, made up and fought again. Friendships grew and broke off. Alliances were made, changed and modified.

The world was like that. Life was like that. And it had some lessons for us. It helped teach us to pick our battles. We learned that we weren't going to win every time, but we could face adversity.

At times, we may have been forced to retreat. We had a code of honor that we lived by, and we tried to uphold it. You only had to defeat your adversary, not necessarily destroy him. And usually, you helped him up when it was over.

We had so many heroes to choose from, to emulate; Robin Hood, William Tell, The Count of Monte Cristo, The Man in the Iron Mask, all tales of swashbuckling chivalry. We watched John Wayne in The Alamo, and The Magnificent Seven with Yul Brenner, Eli Wallach, and Steve McQueen. Our heroes were consistently those who stood with the weak and powerless against the forces of evil, and usually against overwhelming odds.

We fully believed that some things are objectively good, and that some things are objectively evil. In many ways, the world was a lot more black and white than it appears to me, today. Good always conquered evil. The conflict is no longer quite that simple. Our culture has changed. I cannot say if it has changed for good, or for ill, that will be up to the future historians to debate.

It seemed that everyone had some kind of pet. There were always a couple dogs with us when we were out and about. Several neighbor kids had cats. Or, perhaps a little more realistically, they had cats that chose to stay with them. I had a rabbit. His name was Snowball, but Dad of course, had another name for him, Fuzzy Butt. Since Dad had built the rabbit hutch, I guess he could call him whatever he wished.

I took care of Snowball, feeding and watering him and cleaning out his cage when necessary. I entered him into the county fair, and won a First Place Blue Ribbon! I knew he was the best rabbit there. It was nice that others also recognized this fact.

It was fun to let him out in the yard where he would play with our cat. They would stalk each other around the lilac bush, and suddenly pounce when the other came near. It was truly something to see.

There was also a lot going on in the world. The Soviet Union had beaten the US into space with the launch of the Sputnik satellites 1 and 2 in 1957. They could still be seen in 1959, when we moved to Wyoming. And, in Wyoming, there was virtually no light pollution, so it was easy to see, not only the Russian satellite, but also the Milky Way. Dad took us out on the back patio and showed us Sputnik as it circled the Earth above us. All we saw was a tiny blinking light, but on a global scale, that tiny blinking had substantial impact. The Soviet Union had beaten America into space!

In 1960, John F Kennedy defeated Richard M Nixon and was now President of these United State. Mr. Kennedy initiated a number of programs, including exercise programs in schools, the Peace Corps, the Green Beret Special Forces, as well as a substantial number of other civil and social programs. His administration, as well as the time frame in which it was lived came to be known as Camelot, a Golden age in America.

President Kennedy was elected in November 1960, inaugurated in January 1961, and was assassinated by Lee Harvey Oswald in Dallas on November 22, 1963. Vice President Lynden B Johnson was sworn in as President. And so began the War on Poverty, the growth of the War in Viet Nam, as well as the organized protests against our involvement in that war.

In October 1962, President John Kennedy faced down the Soviet Union over the placement of nuclear missiles in Cuba, a scant 90 miles from Florida, and with the capability of striking the East Coast as far north as New York, including Washington, DC. It was a very frightening time for America and the world.

The Cold War was a reality. We dealt with it with weekly "Duck and Cover" drills in the schools. Alarms would sound and the kids would scramble to get under their desks and cover their heads with their arms. I don't think it was designed for much more than to give us a sense of security.

The Civil Rights movement, under the leadership of Martin Luther King, began a rapid growth, as did the Progressive Movement in American politics. The Beat Generation evolved and morphed into the pacifist, anti-Viet Nam War movement that later became the Hippies. Although we did not recognize it at the time, the Social and Cultural Revolution in America had begun.

My folks were known Republicans in a Democratic stronghold, and I paid the price. Several times after President Kennedy's assassination I was challenged and pummeled by other, good Catholic kids at Sts Cyril and Methodius, simply because my parents were Republicans.

In 1964, the average income was $6000 a year, a new home cost $13,500, and a new car cost $3500. President Johnson signed into law the Civil Rights Act of 1964, the Beatles began the British Invasion of music and style, and Mohammed Ali, then known as Cassius Clay, won his first heavy weight title.

In Massachusetts, The Boston Strangler, Albert DeSalvo was captured; Dr. Martin Luther King was awarded the Nobel Peace Prize. The world was changing around us, and we had no real way to anticipate what was to come. The future was coming, whether we were ready for it or not.

Pete, Carrell, and Celia – Point of Rocks Stage Station, WY circa 1960

Kids at play – flat next to house circa, WY 1963

Grandma Canfield with Celia, Tony, and Patricia – Rock Springs, WY

Darrell, Celia, Peter, and Tony – WY circa 1963

Celia, Pete, and Mom – Camping circa 1962

Aunt Nancy and Family visit – Rock Springs, WY circa 1962

The Canfield Family – Sts Cyril & Methodius Catholic Church circa 1961

Darrell, Celia, and Pete – near Gorilla Rock circa 1962

The Valley of the Green River, WY circa 1962

MIDWAY CITY, CALIFORNIA

PART DEAUX

September 1964, we returned to Midway City and the Southern California lifestyle. We were hit with yet another serious case of culture shock. This was certainly not Rock Springs! While in Wyoming, our Midway City home had been rented out, and, when we returned, it had been trashed. Someone had stolen the electrical fixtures, plumbing fixtures, faceplates and anything else they could cart off, including the fruit trees Dad had planted in the yard before we went to Wyoming. Needless to say, Mom and Dad were not happy.

We did a substantial amount of repair work, including painting and replacing most of the things that had been taken. I began scrubbing the walls in the bedroom that was to be mine. The room had been painted a hideous barn red, and, while washing the wall, the paint simply washed off! Dad modified my instructions and told me to wash all of the red paint off of the walls. That was not the result I was hoping for. Who paints a bedroom barn red, anyways?

It was pretty obvious that we were going to have to prime before we painted. Not only had the tenants painted the room an atrocious color, they had used the cheapest paint they could find. What I could not wash off would have to be sealed, or it would bleed through the fresh paint.

This was the year I was in the 6th grade, once again at Midway City Grammar School. The school was a short, 3-block walk from Roosevelt Street. Mike lived down the street and, a block farther up, so did Larry and his brothers. Steve lived just around the corner from Larry.

Sharon lived at the end of our street, but she was in a somewhat different social circle than were my friends, and I although there was some overlap. Although our social cliques were beginning to develop, we weren't yet very exclusive amongst ourselves, nor in our social groupings, either in school or out.

Curiously, I just saw a posting from Sharon on a social media site. It appears from her post that she has had, and is currently living, a good life. I'm pretty sure that it has been over 45 years since we last saw or spoke with one another. I sometimes wonder if others from that neighborhood remember people and events in the same way. I realize that each has his or her own perspective, but is the outline, the shape, the content and context, the same for us all?

Sandy lived about six blocks away, up just past the school… and Sandy was an angel. I was smitten, and the walk was well worth the effort. She was blonde, petite, and beautiful. We fell in love as only children can. She wore my Catholic School ring and we went steady...for most of one day.

My first week in school, I was involved in a disagreement concerning whose turn it was to bat in the noon recess softball game. The disagreement quickly degenerated into a shoving match with Don. To avoid official interference in our negotiations, we arranged to meet after school for what might be termed a "physical negotiation".

Don had gone to school with most of our classmates all of his life. I was the new kid in town. This particular sequence of events turned out to be a necessary contribution to my overall education, and it was well learned.

After school, we did, indeed, meet. Don with his support staff, consisting of his friend Floyd and another supporter whose name eludes me now. But that kid's name really isn't important to the narrative at this point. My friend, Mike, came along. We ended up in someone's back yard, perhaps Floyd's, and Don stepped up and started telling me how much he was going to hurt me, so I hit him.

Amongst other things, I think he thought it unsporting that I should hit him before he had had his say about things. He did seem surprised. Thinking that to be to my advantage, I hit him again, this time in the belly, just as hard as I could. Somehow, he seemed to have lost his enthusiasm for the contest. I had not even been hit, and the fight was over!

Wrong! Floyd stepped up and said that now I would have to fight him. "No, I don't think so", I responded. "We have no reason to fight".

Floyd hit me in the face and said, "OK, now you've got a reason". Not inclined to debate at that time, I just said "OK, let's do it!" I punched him, and their other friend jumped in and swung at me. I ducked, picked up a toy rifle about 4 feet long, with a wooden stock and a steel barrel, and began swinging.

Don ran at me again, and I hit him in the face with the gun. My back swing caught Floyd, and the other guy backed off. I threw down the gun, ran to the fence, jumped up, climbed over and ran toward home.

I came in the back door, hoping to avoid Mom. And promptly ran into Mom, of course. I was a mess. My shirt was torn, I was bruised, my glasses were bent and I had a bloody nose. She of course, was not surprised that I had been in a fight, but she was upset at the blood and tears smearing the dirt on my face.

Now, the first thing Mom wants to do is call the school, the police, the other parents, the newspaper, the parish priest and possibly some Federal Agency in Washington DC to protest this treatment of her son. I suggested to Mom that she might not want to pursue this, as I was sure that I had knocked out, or at least loosened, teeth in the encounter, and there may be other medical and dental issues. Or, other pissed-off parental issues.

In Wyoming, our heroes had been the good guys, the small town Sherriff against the outlaw gang, or the small rancher standing against the big cattle baron. Knights of the Round Table, men with codes of chivalry who understood and honored courage were our role models. In Rock Springs, if 2 kids had a fight, others might watch, but it was between the two protagonists. No one else would even think to join in. In California, however, the consensus seemed to be that 3 to 1 was somehow OK.

I was actually fairly proud of myself in a kind of young, male, machismo way. I had defended myself fairly well against three adversaries. Oh, and my friend, Mike? He sat up on the fence during the entire altercation. I do like to think that he at least cheered for me during the fight. He did help me home after the fact. That was appreciated, and I always intended to thank him for that and for teaching me not to depend on others for my safety, but somehow never got around to it.

One welcome outcome of this event was that it became known that I wasn't a pushover, and that I would fight back. It wasn't something you had to prove often, but it had to be tested and confirmed at least once, just so they knew who I was.

Later, I had to repeat the exercise, only this time it was with a friend. The Pilgrim Boys were from a tight knit family. A fight with any one of them was a fight with all of them. This is how they had been raised.

We were playing some game, when Larry's brother, Johnny, did something to piss me off. There were words, so I swung my fist at him, and connected, rather well, if I do say so myself. He went down, and seemed disinclined to get up.

Next thing I know, Allen is in my face, again telling me of the dire consequences ahead, so we   exchanged punches, and he went down. My friend, Larry is next, and after him, his oldest brother, Tom. I like Larry. He is my friend and don't want to fight him. That however is not an option, they look after one another. It is a family obligation. I really did not want to fight Tom, as he was several years older than were we… and substantially larger!

Just as I am preparing for my battle with Larry, my brother, Darrell, came up from behind me, grabbed my collar, and began dragging me backwards, toward home. He didn't say much, just something along the lines of "OK, the fight's over, let's go home." My fists were still up, and I was ready to continue the fight. No way was I going to back down. I couldn't back down. I still had my pride, you know. "Bring it on!" I thought.

Darrell seemed to think I had fought enough. He had been called at home by one of the neighbors, and it had taken him at least 10 minutes to get there. By the time he got there, I had already been in combat for another 10 minutes or so. There was no quit in me, but I did recognize (and was relieved) that I was being rescued. I just wasn't ready to admit it or to let that relief show. After things cooled off, Larry and I were, again, friends. No offense intended, none taken.

Behind our chain link fence in the backyard was the Field. That was the only name it ever had. And, it was a major part of our daily migrations. We could walk on the street from one friend's house to another, or we could got through the field, climb fences, annoy the older residents who no longer had kids, and, depending on which way you were going, get there substantially faster. The Field was adjacent to both of our homes in Midway City, on Washington Street and on Roosevelt. It became one of our primary routes regardless of where we were going.

The field was a weed filled, power line right-of-way that went all the way to the ocean. There were bike paths and forts. We knew where the mean dogs and grumpy neighbors were, which backyards to avoid, and which we could safely traverse. We knew the backs of homes as well, or better than the fronts.

It was only $.25 to go swimming at the high school pool, which we did often during the summers. I'm pretty well convinced that the parents were willing to give us the quarter just to get rid of us. Parents! Who would ever think that they needed a little peace and quiet without kids around?

Often enough, we would just walk the 2 miles to the high school. There would usually be several of us walking together, and we would meet up with other friends when we got there.

Steve's dad was an Officer in the Navy, stationed at Los Alimitos Navy Station. The base had recreation facilities, including a swimming pool. On rare occasions, we would go to work with his dad, and spend the time in the rec center and swimming pool.

It was at Midway City Grammar School where I met Mr. Gordon, my band teacher. Although I wanted to be a drummer, I had been taking trombone lessons from the Nuns at Saints Cyril and Methodius in Wyoming, simply because we had a trombone and we didn't have a drum.

Mr Gordon continued my musical education teaching me and another horn player to play "To the Colors" for the morning flag ceremony at grammar school. He continued as my Band Instructor when I graduated to Warner Jr. Hi School. At Warner, however, the band marched in local parades, and this allowed us to attend events we might otherwise have missed.

California towns have festivals, fiestas, events and celebrations, almost constantly, if not in one town, then in the next town over. It was not unusual for our Junior Hi School band to participate in 4 or 5 such events each semester, as did most school bands of that era. There were always carnival rides and games of chance at these events, and we tried to take full measure of all of the opportunities, equally presented by the event… such as all the girls from other schools. We were teen-age boys, after all, and puberty was rampant!

There were Cheer Leaders, Pep Squad girls, Dance Teams girls, girls in other school bands, as well as local girls from the communities where the events were being staged. We were so sure of ourselves, sooooo groovy, so outta site, so totally bitchin', and, for a short while, we were in with the in crowd! Gad! We were so young and foolish! But, it truly was an excellent time to be young and foolish.

For each event, we were required to "partner" with one other band member, each to watch out for the other and help keep them out of "trouble". While preparing for one such event, when choosing partners, I told Mr. Neal that I would partner with my friend, Steve. Mr. Neal slowly shook his head and said, "That's not going to happen. Putting the two of you together would be like putting dynamite, gasoline and matches in the same bag, throwing it as high as you can and then waiting to see what happens when it comes down. You two need to find different partners." That was the end of the discussion. Wow. Our reputations had preceded us. I could only wish that we actually were that cool.

Mr. Neal was also my advisor for the Boy Scout Merit Badge in Music. It was he who introduced me to Arthur Fiedler and the Boston Pops Orchestra, giving me an appreciation for a much greater breadth and depth of music with which I might never have become familiar. That appreciation prevails to this day. I still love music, and will as long as I draw breath. As a matter of fact, I am, as I write this, listening to Boston Pops on YouTube.

A thought just occurred to me: do you, my reader in the future, still have YouTube? How do you listen to music? And, what to music do you listen? Today, it is radio, CDs, MP3 players, and vinyl records for true aficionados. A lot of music is streamed over the inter-net. I do hope that one of the things I pass on to future generations will be an appreciation for good music. It is OK to listen to the music of your time, your generation, and your peers.

Artists have been creating music for centuries. Just be aware that there is so much more in the world of music. Don't deprive yourself of it. Take it upon yourself to create opportunities for music in your life. Explore and discover music from other times, other places and other genres other than that with which you are currently comfortable. You might just find a little music you will learn to love. Happy hunting!

At Midway City School, we waited for the teachers to leave at the end of the day so we could claim their cigarette butts from the big ashtray outside the teacher's lounge. The teachers supported our growing habit quite well, thank you very much. They might get only one or two puffs from a cigarette between classes. This left exceptionally long cigarette butts for us, their students. We just had to get there before the janitors cleaned them out.

I always tried to get Mr. Franklin's butts, because they didn't have lipstick on them. All of the women teacher's cigarettes had lipstick on them, and I didn't particularly like the taste of lipstick. A relatively short while later in life, I did get over that particular dislike.

The neighborhood, fairly new at that time, provided us with neighbors. We had the Presley family across the street who claimed to be cousins with Elvis. They were definitely Southern, so they might have been. Who knew? We lived on a cul-de-sac, and were at least nodding friendly with the other families that lived there. Eddie Arnold's brother lived there, and Eddie would occasionally visit.

We did have some neighbors that were a bit... challenging. They were... how can I put this nicely? Oh, well, I guess I really can't--they were poor, white trash. There is no other, better way to put it. City workers were working under the manhole cover in the middle of the street. After her husband went to work, Honey, our neighbor, came out her front door wearing a very short, very sexy, baby-doll pajama. She leaned up against the porch post and struck provocative poses, much to the delight of the city workers!

They also obtained a pair of German Shepherds that I believe they intended to use for breeding. This was before the term "puppy mill" was used to describe breeding dogs for the sole purpose of selling the pups. Their dogs were kept in the back yard, usually in a chain link enclosure that was way too small for these dogs. Consequently, the dogs became mean.

One day while Dad was working in the garden, one of the German Shepherds jumped the fence and attacked our beagle, Duke. Dad, with a shovel in his hand began running toward the dogs. The shepherd was dragging Duke by the scruff of his neck back toward his own yard. When he saw Dad coming at him, he dropped Duke and jumped back into his own yard.

Dad and the neighbor got into a yelling match, and Dad threatened to shoot the dog if it came back into our yard. Mom heard "shoot", thought Dad might actually shoot the dog, and, for good measure, the neighbor too. Mom got scared and called the Sheriff. The dispatcher heard "fight" and "shoot", and the deputies were there almost immediately.

There was one more incident before we moved out of that house and across town to Westminster. Tony and I were playing in the backyard when the German shepherd, having been chained in the back yard, pulled his chain free, jumped the fence into our yard, and came after Tony and me! We were in a corner of the house where we couldn't get past the dog to get away. The dog's chain caught on the fence, but we could not escape past the growling beast! We were terrified!

Darrell heard our yelling, opened the bedroom window and pulled us in. There was another major commotion, with yelling, cursing and threats. Again, the Sheriff was called. Again, the situation was diffused. However, Dad put Darrell in the bedroom window for the next several days with a loaded rifle. His instructions were to shoot any animal that came into the yard, whether with four legs or two.

If you went up our street to Riata, and turned right, you would dead end in the Grammar School. If you turned left on Hazard, and took an immediate right on Newland, it would take you to Warner Junior High School. In California in the mid to late 1960s, Junior High consisted of 7th and 8th grades. High School was 9th grade through 12th.

Junior High was cool, because it wasn't grade school. There were several grade schools represented in each Junior High School in Westminster. There were three Junior High Schools, Warner, Johnson and Stacy. There were people we didn't know who had come from other grade schools, and whatever our status had been in sixth grade no longer existed in Junior High. I was 13 years old when I began Warner Junior High in the fall of 1965.

In some ways, the kids in Wyoming were not that dissimilar from the kids in Southern California. Every segment of society has some sort of pecking order, some social hierarchy or other determinates of status. There were different classifications that we were put into, whether we wished it so or not, most often by our peers, sometimes by the neighborhood in which we lived, occasionally by our parents' vocations and/or their perceived social and economic status.

There were the cool kids that had the very first stingray bicycles, and the first to do wheelies and other tricks on their bikes. They were the junior high school version of "Beautiful People". And then there were the rest of us. We might not have been invited to the cool kid's parties, but we had our own parties. Our folks were as willing as any to take us to the beach, to Trabuco Canyon for a day trip, or overnight camping in O'Neil Park.

Regardless of perceived status, we all went to the school dances. Everyone hoped that their parents would NOT volunteer to chaperone. It was one thing for Steve's Mom to see you try to dance with a girl, and maybe steal a kiss, but if your Mom was the chaperone, you couldn't even try.

My dad was an engineer, Mike's dad was a machinist, Anita's dad was an enlisted Navy lifer, and Steve's dad was a Navy officer. I don't seem to remember Larry's dad at all. He may not have been in the picture, though I do remember his Mom quite well. More often than not, I hung around with Mike, Steve and Larry. We were all in the same Boy Scout troop and attended the same school.

There were, of course, family overlaps. Mike's brother Rocky was occasionally part of Darrell's and Celia's crowd, and sometimes, not. Mike and I, and sometimes his other brothers, Dan and Tim, would go along for the ride. There were also times when Larry's brother, Johnny, would hang around with Mike's brother, Dan. Again, many of us were in Boy Scouts together, and we all went to school together. We were certainly inclusive of everyone in the neighborhood.

The Scout Cabin, a small log cabin, was behind the school, and I'm not sure who owned it, but I would surmise that it was owned by the School District. I seem to recall it being on school property, but I may be mistaken. The Scout Cabin was, however, in constant use. Boy Scout Troops and Girl Scout Troops met in the Cabin, each on different nights. Our Scout Troop met at 5:30 on Tuesday nights. It was where we met up for camping trips, and where we returned when the camping trips ended.

My brother and sister, Darrell and Celia had their group of friends, whom they called the "Termites". I never did know what it meant, and still do not. Celia and Darrell are, respectively 2 years and 4 years older than am I. I was, to a great extent, the kid brother, even though Tony and Patty were growing up behind me.

There was another family down the street that seemed to be integrated into ours. Carol, Kenny, Jerry and Debby were all siblings, roughly equivalent to our family. For a while, Kenny dated Celia, Darrell was interested in Carol, and I had a minor crush on Debby, who is now a Buddhist Nun somewhere in Northern California.

Jerry, as usual, just did without. He was somewhere between Darrell and Celia, but was that gangly, awkward kid found in every crowd. His nickname was, of course, "Charlie Brown". This was in reference to the song of the same name by The Coasters whose chorus kept asking, "Why's everybody always pickin' on me?"

These 2 families were similar in age and number. In our family, there were 2 older teenagers, Darrell and Celia, 1 very young teenager, (that would be me) and 2 kids, Tony and Patty. In their family, there were 3 older teenagers, Kenny, Carol and Jerry, 1 very young teenager, Debby (who was my age), and a younger kid. I don't remember if the kid had a name, but he probably did. It seems that we were either at their house, they were at our house, or we were all at the beach.

There were, of course, others in the social circle, Celia's friends, Leita and Cynthia, and Darrell's friends, Odd John and Tom. Tom later became a US Marine and married Bonnie. In the long run, that did not work out well for either of them, and probably does not need to be in this story. But, there is it, anyway.

When they were at our house, Mom had to come up with a set of rules that applied to everyone.

"Do not use windows as doors. We have 2 perfectly usable doors, one in the living room, and another in the kitchen."

"When entering or exiting through those available doors please remember to open the screen door prior to exiting or entering the residence. Carl has replaced the screen 3 times so far this summer and he has stated that he will take the cost of repair out of the hide of the next person to break a screen door."

"Persons of the opposite sexes shall not both occupy the bathroom at the same time."

"Clothing is required at all times."

"No Over-amorousity!" (I'm pretty sure Mom invented this one)

You get the general idea. Our house seemed to be the place for teens to congregate. Mom and Dad tolerated them. Swimsuits, shorts and t-shirts were the fashion of the day. And, then there was the music. The cars all had AM radios, and most teens had some sort of a record player. Several of the guys thought they played guitar, and all of the girls thought they could sing. There were times, however, when neither of these "thoughts" was an accurate assessment.

I had my circle of friends as well. Mike lived at the end of our street, Larry a couple of streets farther up, and Steve behind Larry. Anita lived across the street and up a couple of houses, and Vivian at the end of the street and across the alley behind Anita's house.

As I said earlier, Anita's dad was an enlisted lifer in the US Navy and pretty down to earth, as were most of the parents in that neighborhood. As

I recall, I think she had one sister and three brothers. In many ways, we were all one big family. Very few of us knocked on anyone's door, we simply let ourselves in.

In the 7th grade, I dated (as much as anyone dated at that time) Vivian. I gave her a gaudy, costume jewelry necklace, with a pink heart. It was an innocent time, and an innocent romance. I don't even remember holding hands with her. The one thing I do remember, though, is that her Dad didn't like me. Of course, he didn't like any male between puberty and senility that may have demonstrated any interest in his daughter whatsoever.

Anita's parents have both now passed, but I did get to see them one last time in about 2007 or 2008. Their memories of me had a lot to do with raiding their refrigerator virtually every time I came over. I was a teenage boy, so of course I was hungry. I was always hungry. They were, at that time, pleased to see me. I was visiting others I had known in that area in Southern California and had just dropped in on them at random. It didn't seem that so many years had passed at all. I am happy that I did so, that I had that final opportunity to see them that one, final time.

Anita's memories were of me helping her burn a huge pot of spaghetti that was supposed to be ready for supper when her folks got home… and hitting me on the head with a Sears catalogue while trying to stop me and another teenager. We were having tricycle races and tricycle demolition derby in their living room. I'm pretty sure that it was for championship of the Galaxy. Then again, it may have been just for the championship of the Solar System. Can't really remember, but it was obviously an important event. I don't think we broke much… but we were smart enough to leave before her Dad got home.

I enjoyed the Junior High dances, the sock hops; although I don't think I actually asked a girl to dance in the 7th grade. I was pretty good at holding up the back wall of the auditorium and looking across the room at the girls. It was, at that age, socially acceptable to meet up with, and talk with, whomever was there.

This is probably when Mom decided that I needed to take dance lessons from Miss Karolyn's Dance Emporium. I was not thrilled at the prospect. Come on, now. Girls are graceful and dance. Guys are not graceful, especially young, teenage guys. They are, as Mom used to say, "…Like a bull in a china shop…" They break things and they cuss. And, guys really shouldn't cuss around girls.

It was several years later before I recognized the value of that particular gift from my folks. Over time and in subsequent interactions with female, girl persons, of the tender gender, those dance lessons have, more than once, proven their value.

Mom and Dad also thought it important that we should all be introduced to the social graces. Manners, courtesy and decency are the things that indicate that one has culture. It had value, and it was noticed that we knew how to conduct ourselves in "polite company".

We were taught to hold the door for others, to make eye contact while shaking hands, to use the words "please" and "thank you". Manners, we were taught, are a social lubricant, based on mutual respect, allowing social and business interactions to flow much more easily. Thanks, Mom and Dad. I really do appreciate it.

I remember the music, it was everywhere! We enjoyed Rock n' Roll, ballads, folk music, swing, Beach music, and much more. There were the Ventures, the Beatles, Janis Joplin, Stone Pony, Bobby Sherman, Peter, Paul and Mary and so many more. The music was, and continues to be, the sound track of our lives.

Bobby Vinton sang "Melody of Love", the Righteous Brothers, and "Unchained Melody". Sgt Barry Sadler sang the "Ballad of the Green Berets", and Johnny Rivers, "The Poor Side of Town". In 1966, Frank Sinatra was in the Top 40 with "Strangers in the Night", while his daughter, Nancy, also had a Top 40 hit, "These Boots Are Made for Walking".

The 1960s were the era of the British Invasion, when the music and culture of England was brought to the US with the Beatles, the Rolling Stones, Petula Clark, the Dave Clark Five and so many, many others. The musical variety, American and British, was virtually limitless!

There was something incredibly special for a teenage boy, holding your girl close, swaying to the music... hoping she cannot hear your heart pounding in your chest...nor hear you counting your steps as you dance. In many so ways, that music, that time, created a magical social structure around which our young lives were being created. I believe that for many of this generation, that music, that vibe, that sense of whom we were, and who we are continues through to this day.

We were fortunate to have been young in that time of music, fashion and style. Our generation had a sense of style unlike any before that time or since. Paisley was everywhere, as were pseudo-military styles. Hats were prevalent, with berets in various colors making their own fashion statement. Bell bottom pants were found on men and on women, and many wore vests, both leather vests and sweater vests.

Color, beautiful, vibrant color was everywhere! Flower power was in full bloom, and everything was in color. Oh, and did I mention miniskirts? We discovered that girls had legs, and they went all the up to . . . . . there!

Plaid was so very "in", with plaid pants, plaid jackets and plaid suits. Smoking jackets were popularized by Hugh Hefner, and if you were really with it, you also had a couple of pastel turtleneck shirts to wear under your sports coat. We were so groovy!

Darrell, Celia, Pete, Tony, and Patty – circa 1964

The Termites – Midway City, CA circa 1966

JUNIOR HIGH

In December 1966, we moved from Midway City to a new home in Westminster, a distance of about 4 miles. This was just about the mid-point of my 8th Grade year. Due to that move, I was, once again, the new kid. I transferred from Warner Junior High to Stacey Junior High, and graduated from Stacey in 1967. While attending Stacy, I met different people and became friends with some.

While at Stacey, I continued in the band, which at least gave me some basis for forming relationships. Other than the kids in my neighborhood, I really do not remember many of the names or faces of Stacey alumni. The second half of 8th grade was a mere 5 months, at which point we would all move to our respective high schools. Some of these new friends would go to Westminster High School, in Westminster, and some would go to Marina High School in Huntington Beach.

Judi was one whom I did not meet at Stacy, but we were introduced later, subsequent to junior high, by a mutual friend Diane Rasmussen. I am afraid that her name is all that I remember of Diane… and perhaps the fact that it was she who introduced me to Judi.

Judi had gone to Stacey, and later went to Marina High School. Consequently, Marina was where I went to school dances… With Judi, of course. Judi was my sweetheart during my junior year of high school. We went on dates, with either her parents or mine driving us, to whatever the event may have been: the beach, the movies, a school dance, whatever. We got a little tired of having parents around all the time, but it was pretty much our only option, at that time. There was no way her father was EVER going to allow her to ride on the back of my motorcycle!

Judi's parents had an in-ground swimming pool in the backyard. Her dad, however, did not want us to use the pool in the backyard. He never really liked me. As a simple matter of fact, he just barely tolerated me. He certainly did not want me in the pool with his daughter wearing swimming suits, especially when no one else was home. The swimming suits simply did not cover enough skin for his tastes, and he was never totally sure that we kept the swimming suits on, anyway. One phrase I would never, ever have used in his hearing range would be "Skinny dipping".

Judi was heavily invested in her youth group at the Westminster Presbyterian Church. This gave us many more options, as the youth group organized outings for the teens and provided bus transportation to a variety of events. The youth group members were encouraged to invite other teens.

With the youth group, we went to Knott's Berry Farm and to Pacific Ocean Park, known locally by its initials, P. O. P. On these outings, the chaperones couldn't possibly be everywhere, so, some of the kids (not ME, of course), may have shared a stolen kiss . . . or two . . . or three. Of course, I can neither confirm nor deny if anything ever happened at all!

Our paths have crossed from time to time over the years, and we remain friendly to this day. As a matter of fact, at my request, Judi sent a birthday card to my Dad this year for his 85th birthday. It's that kind of a friendship, very close in a distant sort of way. At some point, as we grew up and grew apart, the romance faded away, and a lifelong friendship has developed. For this, I am grateful.

SUMMER ON THE RANCH

Our family went on vacation every summer, usually to visit Dad's parents on the family farm, some 40 miles west of Spokane, Washington. He planned it so he was there to help with the summer farm work that needed to be done, and that his Dad might have trouble getting done. He enjoyed visiting with his folks and friends still in the area, and he enjoyed the farm work.

We kids enjoyed it as something totally different from our lives in California. We went to the lake as opposed to the ocean. We rode horses instead of bicycles. There were barns and out buildings to explore. One summer Dad gave me his archery set from his childhood to hunt rats and other rodents in the chicken coop. I'm afraid that I wasn't very successful. I shot a lot of arrows, but I don't think I actually hit a single rodent. I really wasn't a very good hunter.

There were also times to sit in the shade on the grassy front yard and listen to the older folks talk about their lives, of events that had happened during the course of their lives. Dad, born in 1932, was a young boy during World War II and a teenager when it ended. During the war, there was a pervasive fear of the Japanese invading the American West Coast.

Dad's family developed plans on what to do and where to go in the event that an invasion was actually to happen. Their go-to point was the old water cistern in the fold of the hill behind the barn.

Not every summer played out the way it was planned. For example, there was that summer when we all came down with chicken pox; five kids, all sick and bedridden, all running fevers, all requiring care. That was not my favorite summer. I'm pretty sure it was not Mom's favorite summer at the farm, either.

While playing in the barn we climbed the haystacks, built forts with hay bales, and invented new uses for hay. On one such occasion, Darrell, on top of the stack, yelled, "Look out, below!" as he rolled a bale over the edge. The 65-pound hay bale landed on me and totally knocked the wind out of me! I wasn't moving and poor Darrell thought he had killed me. He just knew Mom would not be happy with that outcome. I am, however, reasonably sure that I survived.

Summer of 1967, between Junior High and High School, I spent working on the family farm in Eastern Washington State, near the small town of Davenport. I also worked for a couple of the neighboring farms.

My day was spent bucking hay bales and doing other assorted farm jobs as assigned; slopping pigs, feeding chickens, gathering eggs from the hen house and shoveling shit. Literally, shoveling shit. I had to clean out barns and stalls, some almost knee deep in horseshit, mule shit, chicken shit, and other kinds of shit. It was part of the job, and I was pretty good at it. This experience helped prepare me for future government jobs later in my life.

I rode a horse for Elman's spring cattle roundup. Cattle were rounded up from all corners of the ranch, the young bulls castrated and the yearlings branded. Admittedly, for the most part, I just tried to stay on top of the horse and keep moving in the same general direction as everybody else.

My job was to ride slowly back and forth behind the bunched cattle, keeping them drifting in the general direction of the corrals where the branding and castrating was done. And, for Pete's sake, don't do anything loud or sudden! We do not need a stampede!

The other, older hands chased the cattle out of the creek beds and out of small treed areas. My job was to ride slowly back and forth, keeping the cattle slowly drifting toward the main ranch. It took most of a week to get them in the branding pens and the best part of another week branding and castrating.

I remember well the sounds and the smells, the yelling cowboys, the bawling calves, the heat and the excitement. The ranch dogs helped work the cattle, nipping at their heels. My friends in California could not even picture what I had been doing on the farm. I rather felt sorry for them.

And then, there were the piglets. The rancher's prize sow had had two litters of piglets, one right after the other. The first litter had not yet weaned, so the sow would only nurse the first, and ignored the second litter. They should have been weaned, but, alas, not yet.

My boss, the owner of the ranch, decided that we should capture and separate the two litters. This involved chasing piglets all over the pig corral and stuffing them into old burlap feed sacks. There were, as I remember, around eight piglets in each litter. There were only five of us, and so we were severely outnumbered. And, there were times that I thought that the pigs were smarter than we were. There were also times when I was sure that the piglet count was not eight plus eight, but eight times eight!

Now for those who are unfamiliar with pigs, they are VERY fast, and can turn on a dime and give you 35 cents change. Every time you opened the sack to put a pig in, one of those previously captured would try to escape, and often succeeded.

If you were to slip and fall in the mud in the pigpen, they would all get out. If you ran into one of the other hands chasing pigs, they all got away, both yours and his, and we had to catch them again. Good Lord, we were laughing so hard that we could barely stand!

Boss promised a $10 bounty to whoever caught the most pigs. I made a claim of 50 pigs caught, but of course, the boss wouldn't count the "caught and escaped piglets", only the total number of pigs in your sack at the end of the day. By suppertime, we had caught them all, put the older piglets in a separate enclosure, the second litter with the momma sow. We were filthy, sweaty, hungry, and exhausted! But, we had definitely accomplished something! Again, the city kids I'd left behind in California just didn't know what they were missing.

I remember spending something in the neighborhood of $10 that summer to buy a transistor radio from the Five and Dime department store in Davenport. The song I remember from that summer was "Silence is Golden", by the Tremelos. Grandma C was appalled, appalled, I say, at my waste of money. "You should have saved that money for college!"

All in all, it was a good summer for me. I was paid $20 a day, plus room and board. I slept in the bunkhouse, and ate at the big table with the family and farm hands, and used the outhouse, when necessary. I had grown up quite a bit over the summer, put on a bit of muscle, and I felt good about myself. I had done a man's job for 7 or 8 weeks. I was going home, and I was going home with money in my pocket, my own money, that I had earned of my own hard labor.

Since Dad worked for the railroad, I could ride the train from Spokane, Washington to Los Angeles on his rail pass. And, I could, and did, ride it by myself. Yes sir, I was 14 years old, and, I WAS all that...and a bag of chips.

I got home and returned to my Southern California, beach bum lifestyle. My friends were close, the beach was right there where I had left it, and there was still a bit of summer left before school began. Life was, indeed, good. I'm afraid that, back then, I didn't even realize how good I had it!

Pete on Dad's horse – Peewee, Davenport, WA circa 1965

Pete with scythe – circa 1967

SAINT ANTHONY'S HIGH SCHOOL

I was looking forward to going to Westminster High School with my peers, but my parents had other plans. They believed that I would receive a better education in a private, Catholic high school. They enrolled me in Saint Anthony's College Prep High School for Boys, on 7th Street in Long Beach, California.

There was also a Saint Anthony's College Prep High School for Girls, co-located with the Boy's School, with many of the activities between the 2 schools being co-ed. Although most classes were gender segregated, the band, choir, cheerleaders and school dances were gender integrated. My problem was, again, I was an outsider. Most of the other students at Saint Anthony's had matriculated from the Long Beach and Los Angeles County Catholic grade school system, and had been gender segregated only since entry into high school.

In other words, they knew each other, and had for a substantial period of time. I knew no one at Saint Anthony's, male or female. My friends were in Orange County, and Saint Anthony's was not. Saint Anthony's is in Long Beach, and Long Beach is in Los Angeles County.

I'm reasonably convinced that it may not have been so bad if I had been sent to Mater Dei, the Catholic high school in Orange County. I would have had substantially more common ground with the kids from suburban Orange County than I had with the inner city kids of Long Beach.

The two schools were, in large measure, run by and taught by people in religious orders. The girls were taught by nuns, and the boys by Franciscan brothers. In actuality, there was really only one school, with internal divisions between the religious Brothers and Sisters and gender segregation. Neither the nuns nor the Brothers were inclined to suffer any nonsense from students.

The school was empowered by parents to utilize corporal punishment as a part of the educational process, with the understanding that it would be administered in a manner proportionate to each student's particular, secular, violation. It occurs to me now, that penance was administered not only for religious sins, but for secular trespasses, as well. And, I might add, administered with a certain degree of enthusiasm on the part of the staff.

Although a good, solid smack in the back of the head for just being a knucklehead required no justification what so ever. "He was a being a knucklehead, so I smacked him", the brothers might say. Quite obviously, this was a necessary and effective methodology to keep us on track with our studies and with our comportment. We were, after all, teenage boys.

Anyways . . . I lasted through my freshman and sophomore years at SA. After my sophomore year, I left rather as a matter of mutual consent and benefit. I did not want to be there, and I really don't think that they wanted me there anymore, either. Once again, I'm pretty sure that I was being a "dirty elephant".

The one friend I made at Saint Anthony's, Ken, is still a friend to this day. He too, sent a card to my Dad on his 85th birthday.

Ken was a rather rebellious soul, although that was not an uncommon affliction among Southern California's young people in the late 1960s. We were all just a bit rebellious. He and I skipped school one day to go hang out in downtown Long Beach, smoke cigarettes, go to the beach and perhaps play some pool at the Golden Cue Pool Hall.

I called the school, acting the part of Ken's father, excusing his absence. Ken was going to call as my father, excusing my absence. It was the perfect plan. I managed to lower my voice enough to pull it off, but when it was Ken's turn to call the school, about half way through the conversation, he started laughing and couldn't finish the call.

He got away with ditching for the day, but I got an in-school suspension - - - on SATURDAY - - - FOR 8 HOURS! Didn't they tell you about those child labor laws? It was a private Catholic School, so we could VOLUNTEER, or BE volunteered, as much as we wished. Scrub floors, paint classrooms, clean the bathrooms, and clean the church, gardening and grounds keeping. Whatever needed to be done, some miscreant student on detention would be "Volunteered" to address it.

I and a couple other St. Anthony miscreant scholar/volunteers had been given the task of painting the interior of a nearby small house owned by the school. During the school year, it was rented to one of the young, single, male teachers employed by the school.

I was on a ladder about half way through a cigarette when one of the Brothers came in to check on our progress. I saw him first, and quickly dipped my cigarette into the bucket of paint. He seemed to sniff the air as he came in, but the intense shine from my halo must have blinded him to the fact that someone in that house had been smoking. Getting caught smoking was probably good for three or four more Saturday detentions!

Ken had made a couple of decisions, using very limited judgment, the consequences of which resulted in his "Volunteering" to go to San Francisco for the summer, working as janitor in an inner city, Catholic school. Where the school was located had never been a good part of San Francisco, but it wasn't much worse than most other big cities. He survived. I would assume that he learned whatever lesson it was that they wanted him to learn. I guess I'll have to ask him when next we speak, just what it was that he learned from this particular experience.

Ken's parents didn't want Ken hanging out with me, because I was a bad influence. My parents didn't want me hanging out with Ken, because he was a bad influence. He and I continued to hang out and have a good time together, just bad influencing the hell out of each other!

I have to admit that the education I received at Saint Anthony's was a superior education. As much as I rebelled against being there, I became educated in spite of myself. Mr. Latham taught me how to write a coherent sentence.

Brother August taught a course in Ethics, a subject seldom broached in the arena of public education. There truly are things that are objectively good, and things that are equally, objectively evil.

Brother Charles, a prior California Golden Gloves Boxer helped teach us to pick our fights much more judiciously. I observed a cocky young man challenge him. This was not a judicious decision.

Brother Joseph, a quiet, contemplative man, my Biology teacher, showed me that I was actually much brighter than I had given myself credit for. Mr. Gonzales taught me much more Spanish then either he or I recognized at the time.

These men, dedicated to the education of the succeeding generation, made a difference in my life, and, I am sure, in the lives of many more young men in a time of social turmoil.

I will admit to a much greater appreciation of Saint Anthony's now than I could have mustered at that time. As much as I fought it, that school contributed much to the betterment of my life ever since.

WESTMINSTER

I was finally allowed to transfer to Westminster High School for my Junior Year. Returning to the public school system was both a blessing and a curse. I again got to go to school with friends who lived in the neighborhood. We had always hung out together, even while going to different schools. I had even attended some of the Westminster High School events, such as football and basketball games.

Because I had gone to two of the Junior High Schools that fed into Westminster, I knew kids from both. In some ways, however, I was again the new guy. My absence from Westminster had allowed others in the class to bond and to develop relationships during those important first two years of high school. This seems to be when and where social skills and social circles were born, nurtured and matured.

I had, to some degree missed that mass immersion into puberty that my peers in public school had experienced. Such things as puberty were severely frowned upon and mightily discouraged at Saint Anthony's. That is not however, to suggest that I was not, at least interested in puberty, but I just hadn't had much opportunity to explore it in any real depth.

I remember a party that Wes hosted in his parent's home. He had spent the previous couple of weeks listening to 33 rpm, long play, record albums, and re-recording them on his reel-to-reel tape system. When he was done, he had a full six or eight hours of music in the order he thought would work best for his party.

Many of the kids, boys and girls, liked their hair long, and some wore it short, but it was always neat, perfectly styled and combed. We wore bell-bottom trousers and polyester shirts, Nehru jackets and paisley. The girls wore dresses or skirts and blouses, often accessorized with the required thin headband. Whatever the occasion happened to be, we certainly made it a point to dress for it. We had style, grace and class. We were so very groovy!

Much of the styles of the day had come from Carnaby Street, along with the music of the British Invasion. Turtleneck sweaters and miniskirts were all the rage. And most girls had more than one pair of go-go boots. Men's shirts had butterfly collars, stretching nearly to the shoulder. Other fashions incorporated American Indian aspects, including fringed buckskins and leather headbands. Moccasins could be found everywhere, and could be in everything from loafers to knee length. Whatever the style, whatever the fashion, we made it look GOOD!

Wes and I played around on guitars, trying to learn the songs of the day. Wes became a pretty good musician, but I never pursued it enough to actually play anything. Later, after high school, Wes performed as a lounge singer, playing at Westminster Lanes, a bowling alley. Since they paid him to show up and play, I guess that means that he was a professional musician. Wes kind of reminded me of Billy Joel's "Piano Man". Except, of course, Wes didn't play piano, he played guitar. I'm pretty sure he couldn't carry a piano to the gig in his Fiat.

He and I did manage to learn one rendition of Scarborough Faire together that we didn't destroy too badly. A memory that he and I share is sitting on the brick planter in front of my parent's home, playing it over and over, trying to get it right. We actually got close a time or two. At least, WE didn't think we sounded too bad.

Wes' Dad owned a beauty shop in Belmont Shores. Once in a while over the summer between sophomore and junior Years, Wes and I would catch a ride with his Dad into Belmont Shores. We would walk over to nearby Naples Bay and spend the day on the sand and in the water. We met and became friends with a number of other teenage kids, who were also spending summer at that beach.

It wasn't too bad, all in all. You could buy hamburgers for 15 cents and a Coke, a Pepsi or Nehi Grape or Orange was only a dime. A nickel candy bar cost, you guessed it, a nickel. Fifty cents a day would pretty much see us through. We were, of course, hungry when we got home. That's just how teenage boys are, after all, hungry, always hungry.

After several such trips, Wes and I managed to introduce ourselves to a couple of girls from Long Beach who also spending the summer at Naples Bay. We enjoyed each other's company, but it never became a romantic thing for any of us. We liked the girls, and they liked us. We teased them, and they teased us, but it never developed into anything other than friendships. We spent that one summer together, but after summer, the friendships simply faded away. I'm afraid I can't even remember their names, nor would I know them if I ran into them today.

Mom and Margie had known each other since childhood and throughout their high school years in the 1930s. They had maintained their friendship over the intervening years, even before the inter-net and social media made it so much simpler.

They wrote letters by hand in which they shared each other's lives. Each envelope sent was marked on the outside with the letters "C P O F U A F B". Mom had once called Margie her chum, a phrase picked up from British sailors she met during World War II when she worked in Navy Supply. When Margie looked up the term "chum" in the dictionary, she saw that the first definition was "Chopped Pieces of Fish, Used as Fish Bait". Margie was highly offended! It was the second definition that identified a "chum" as a friend or companion. In later years, however it became one of many family stories to be passed down.

Rick was Margie's son. He was in the Navy and stationed at the Long Beach Naval Station. When not on duty, my folks allowed him to stay in our extra bedroom. His ship would soon be putting to sea. Rick, like so many other young men, was on his way to Viet Nam. When he left, his Honda 160cc motorcycle remained in our garage. Somehow, by some miracle, it became mine! I like to think that my folks had some arrangement with Rick, but I was allowed to ride it. And, ride it, I did! Life was GOOD!

I covered a large part of Southern California on that small bike. Because Lynn spent summers at her mother's house in Santa Monica, and the school year with her father in Westminster, I would make that journey from Westminster to Santa Monica once or twice a week.

It was an 80 mile round trip, but gas was only 30 cents a gallon. The cost for the round trip was less than a dollar. A couple of times, I took my friend, Mike along for the ride. More often than not, however, I made the trip alone.

On another occasion, I had picked up Meri, another friend, and we were on our way to some event. I was riding the Honda, and Meri was on the back. As we rode along Westminster Ave, there was a small patch of sand, left over from painting the stripes on the road. Just as I hit that patch of sand, the car in front of us stopped suddenly. I could not stop and ran into the back of the car.

In doing so, I managed to slam my genitals against the gas tank and speedometer. I staggered to the curb, out of the street, put the bike on its kickstand, fell to the ground curled up in a fetal position and passed out.

Each time I awoke, Meri was standing over me asking "Where does it hurt, Pete, where does it hurt?" I could not stand, I could not breathe. I sure as hell could not carry on a conversation.

Meri called Miss Karolyn to tell her what had happened. My mom happened to be visiting Karolyn, so Mom got the message and called Dad. Dad arrived shortly after a policeman had shown up. The officer was standing over me asking questions.

Dad shoved the cop out of the way and picked me up, carrying me like a baby. The officer said he wasn't done with his questions. Dad said "The Hell you aren't. If you have any more, we will be in the emergency room at Westminster Hospital. Now get the hell out of my way!" The cop did just that, he got out of Dad's way.

I ended up in the hospital overnight for observation, and an appointment scheduled for a week out. I am in overwhelming pain, can barely stand. When I walk, it is with my legs as far apart as possible, and leaning on a walking stick. My scrotum was swollen to the size of a grapefruit!

As I am standing in the hall outside the doctor's office after my checkup, I heard the doctor tell my mom that I had developed a blood clot in my scrotum, and it had to be evacuated! I was not a doctor, but I knew what they meant!

They were going to cut into my scrotum! NO! I have had fun before, and it was absolutely nothing like they had planned for me. That was definitely not on my social schedule over the next few months. I wasn't going to let them do it!

Well, I did, and they did, and the rest of my summer was ruined. I was afraid that they might take the wrong thing, and I would never be a father. They got the right thing, however, and a short six or seven weeks later (that took an eternity or two) I was almost walking upright again.

We again headed north for our annual summer vacation trek. I rode in the back of the camper and had no desire to stand or walk, or do much of anything.

I rode that Honda 160 all over Southern California for just over a year. On his return trip from Viet Nam, Rick's ship had stopped off in Japan, where he bought a couple more, larger motorcycles. He really didn't seem that concerned about my little Honda.

I had ridden it pretty hard over the past year, and eventually sold it to the Pilgrim boys for $100. I didn't have the title, of course, but their plan wasn't to register it, but to turn it into an off-road, dirt bike. I spent that $100 buying my first car, a 1960 Peugeot 403.

I bought my Peugeot from Rickie's dad. Rickie's dad was our neighborhood mad scientist in Midway City. He drove a steam powered Jaguar sports car and had a steam powered VW van. It seemed he was always tinkering in his garage or backyard shop. I think he held patents on some of his inventions from which he received residual payments, so didn't really have a "job" that he went to every morning and came home from every night. He seemed to always be working in his shop, talking to himself and puttering around, until he blew up himself and his shop. It may not have been the first explosion there, but it was his last. He had a really nice funereal, and there was a pretty good turnout from the neighbors for the wake.

That Peugeot was so very cool. It had a 4 cylinder, 65 horsepower motor, with a 4-speed transmission on the steering column. Mine was black in color, a touring model with seats, that, when slid all the way forward, could lay down to merge into a large, flat sleeping area. It had a sunroof that slid open to let the sun shine in.

If the battery ever died, the car came equipped with a hand crank. I would get out in front, raise the bonnet to prime the carburetor, and twist the crank. It only took two or three tries before the engine would catch, sputter and then, finally, run. There is a specific technique to hand-cranking an engine to start it, but the technique is easily learned. I learned it on my way home from buying it, when the car stalled in the middle of the largest intersection in town, Beach Boulevard and Westminster Avenue.

I got out of the car, raised the bonnet, and began cranking. Cars were honking, drivers were laughing, and kids in back seats were pointing at me. I was so very pleased that I could entertain so many people with so little effort. I felt like an idiot, and if the term had existed at that time, I might even have had "buyer's remorse".

I felt like an idiot, I was pissed off, I felt like an idiot, I was embarrassed, I felt like an idiot, and I was sure that everyone I knew was going to drive by. And, Oh yeah, I felt like an idiot! Everyone would know that I was that weird guy cranking his car in the middle of Westminster and Beach Boulevard. Cranking a car?!? Seriously? C'mon, this is 1968, we don't start cars with a hand crank any more. But, I do.

I dated several girls throughout high school, but only a couple exclusively, and on reflection, not for very long periods of time. Most of these relationships seemed to last for about a year, or perhaps just a little less, perhaps a little more. And, some that were on again, off again, and, occasionally, on again.

With a couple of the girls I knew in my teens, we may have dated in the beginning, but we have evolved into long-term, and in a very few instances, lifelong, friendships.

I also had friends who were only girls, incidentally. Their gender had little to do with their ability to have fun doing other things. Also, during this time, when not busy with school, or doing "guy" things, I was active in Miss Karolyn's Creative Arts Studio.

At that time in America, dance was considered to be for girls, and if guys liked it, they must be a little, "girly". However, the ratio of girls to guys was about 10:1. This statistic did not offend me. I rather appreciated it.

Miss Karolyn taught dance, etiquette, manners and culture. She taught ladies to be ladies, and she taught young men to be young gentlemen. She taught ballet, tap, ballroom, tango, etc. I took modern dance, and had, previously, taken some ballroom lessons from her. I also learned very basic ballet, essentially the first 4 positions, and some of the vernacular.

My mom worked with Miss Karolyn, doing paperwork for the business, while Miss Karolyn took care of the "artistic" side of things. I got teased at school by some of the "jocks", but pointed out that they were hanging out in the locker room with sweaty guys, while I was spending my time with cute girls in leotards. I knew who had the better deal.

Pete Canfield – circa 1966

Pete in derby and sweater vest – circa 1967

My first car – 1960 Peugeot

Mary, Marlene, Lynn, Ruth - Miss Karolyn's Create Arts Studio circa 1968

Volkswagen Van circa 1968

MARY

It was summer of 1968, and Mary and I had plans to go do... something. I can't remember where we were going, but we were on our way. We were in Huntington Beach, heading toward Fountain Valley. We must have been all of 16 years old. I had my driver's license, but did not yet have a car, so Mary's Mom, Karolyn, loaned us her Volkswagen van. It was that archetypical barn red and off- white VW van, ubiquitous in Southern California in the 60s. It was typical of the times, with an underpowered, four cylinder, air-cooled engine, and a sloppy, manual, 4-speed transmission on the floor.

Anyway, we were enjoying a warm, summer, Southern California night, in a car borrowed from her mother, listening to music on the AM radio, probably 93 KHJ. We were visiting, laughing and enjoying each other's company, when her Mom's car simply stopped running. The engine died, and there we were.

We had no idea what to do. For several moments we sat and just stared at each other. We finally decided that the best course of action was for Mary to stay with the van, and for me to walk to a phone booth and call her Mom. Yeah, a phone booth. There were no cell phones, there were no laptop computers, electronic tablets or I-pads, but phone booths were everywhere. All you needed to make a call was a dime.

With no other choice, no other option, I began walking until I found a phone booth at a convenience store. Got there, didn't have a dime to make the call. I went into the store to ask for change for a dollar. The clerk said he could only make change if I bought something. OK, I didn't really want it, but I spent a nickel on a candy bar, got the change, and returned to the phone booth. I picked up the receiver, and . . . . . no dial tone, out of order! I stepped out of the phone booth and looked up and down the street. I could see the lights of another store just a bit farther down the street. I started walking in that direction.

I got to the next store, found the pay phone, and called Karolyn told her where I was and what had happened. She agreed to come rescue us. I found a place to sit down on the brick planter in front of the store, and waited. Karolyn shows up about a half hour later. OK, time to get back to Mary and the car. By now, Mary has been sitting alone in the van for an hour and a half, anxiously awaiting my return.

I can't remember where the van is! I can't even remember how I got HERE! I had walked, changed directions more than once, had gone into two stores and had gotten myself turned around. Karolyn is becoming less and less patient... and more vocal.

She started accusing me of selling her car across the border and her daughter to white slavers! The more she lost it, the more upset she got, the more vocal she became, and the more vocal she became, the more confused I got about where the van was. The only thing I did know was that it was on the downside of an overpass over the 405 freeway, somewhere. I think the van was facing east...or maybe, south... or… something.

We circled the vicinity for what seemed several eternities, and finally, finally spotted the car. But, we were on the wrong side of a divided road, had to go down a couple of blocks to get turned around and come back to the van.

OK, I had sold neither the van nor her daughter. Karolyn was still, decidedly, not happy with either of us, but she was no longer threatening me with traumatic neutering with a chain saw. I appreciated that.

Mary had waited, more or less patiently, for most of 3 hours. It just didn't seem that we were meant to be anything more than just the best of friends. We did, and do, love one another. We were simply not "In Love". It never did develop into any kind of romance, but we remain friends and in touch to this day, some 50 years later. I don't think Karolyn ever again loaned her car to me. And, I really don't think I ever again asked her to.

LYNN

Then, there was Lynn. Lynn was, and still is, an exotic, darkly beautiful, mysterious woman of Italian heritage. Her olive complexion, always tanned, her hair dark. She was slim, elegant and graceful. When she danced, my heart danced.

All I had to do was to win her away from Rob, who currently laid claim to her affections. I proceeded to do just that, to win her away. He really wasn't her type, anyways. Her type was, purely by coincidence . . . . . me!

I complimented her and flattered her and charmed her to the greatest extent of my ability. Did I mention that Lynn was, and is, beautiful?

I achieved my goal, I won her over. Lynn's heart was mine, and mine was most definitely hers. I chased her until she caught me!

We went to the movies, to high school football and basketball games and high school dances, to the beach, to Disneyland and to Knott's. We swam in her swimming pools, both in Westminster and in Santa Monica.

Lynn was an integral and active part of the Westminster High School Drama Department, so I went to those productions, as well. Of course I was interested, Lynn was in it, wasn't she? Additionally, I had various other friends in the Drama Department, Mary and Meri, Rob and George, Sande and Theresa, all of whom played roles in my story, some with small parts, some greater.

Among other productions, the Drama Department presented a fascinating, student written, multi-media, live stage show, entitled "Garbage, and Other Facts of Life". I remember it well. I helped Lynn and Mary tie-dye t-shirts for that show. Locally, it was considered to be very controversial, garnering both rave reviews and stern, disapproving criticism.

The show was about contemporary social issues, including the Viet Nam War, social and civil rights, social and civil disobedience, protests, patriotism and false flags. I thought it to be very well done. But, then again, Lynn was in it, wasn't she? Of course it was good. Did I mention that Lynn is beautiful?

Lynn spent the school year living in Westminster with her Dad and Step-Mom. She spent summers in Santa Monica with her Mom and Step-Dad. Both homes had swimming pools in the back yard, and both were very nicely furnished. Her parents had a sense of class, of elegance and of style, and they passed that on to their daughters. It gave me cause to refine my own manners, and to be on my best behavior when I visited, so as not to seem uncultured. Again, thank you, Mom. Thank you, Dad, for insisting I take those dance lessons in 7th grade.

I remember taking Lynn to the ballet "Gisele". Lynn was a dancer, as well as an actor; ballet, tap, jazz, ballroom and swing, she was adept and graceful in all of them. It required a fair amount of effort on my part to keep up with her, but I was motivated. Did I mention that she is beautiful?

She was a participant in Miss Karolyn's Creative Arts Studio, and a major part of the reason that I was also a participant. There was a fine, delicate femininity about her that intrigued and terrified me. While I was not yet of an age to appreciate her in every aspect, I was well aware that other guys were probably interested in her, at least the ones that weren't blind. She was beautiful. Just as I had won her affection, I knew that other guys might wish to do the same. But, just because I was aware of it didn't mean I had to like it.

One very specific date with Lynn stands out from among the rest. We went to Farrell's Old Time Ice Cream Parlor on Beach Boulevard in Huntington Beach. First, we enjoyed way more ice cream than we needed. Then our conversation devolved into social and political discussion.

This time the subject was abortion and we were on opposite sides of the debate. The discussion became heated, and had the potential of damaging our romance. It ruined the date, but we did save the relationship.

I'm pretty sure that I modified my view to be more aligned with hers. And, as I mature, I now realize that she was right. I'm not surprised. Did I mention that she is beautiful? She was also very smart, with wisdom beyond her years. It was my good fortune to have her as a part of my life, even though that time was, in retrospect, brief.

There was a warm summer evening that I remember fondly. It was after midnight, and obviously way too late to be visiting. That alone would not, and did not deter me. It was clearly too late to ring the doorbell, as her parents would be the ones to answer, and that was not who I was desirous of seeing. Especially did not want to see them after ringing their doorbell at some time after midnight. I was astute enough to know that they were apt to be less than welcoming. It was not too late, however, to gently throw pea gravel against her upstairs bedroom window in an attempt to awaken her.

Did I mention that Lynn was beautiful? But never so lovely as that beautiful, magnificent 16 year old girl, framed in the window, illuminated by the full moon on a warm, sultry, summer's night. Of such moments are created the dreams of youth, and the sweet memories of age. It was a long time ago, a more innocent time, and I remember it well with bittersweet, tattered remnants of leftover love. Thank you, Lynn.

Lynn and I continued to be a couple for the most part until I went into the Army. I don't think I can claim Attention Deficit Disorder, but I most certainly was not paying attention. I let her slip away. It was only later in life that I realized the value in what I had left behind.

Remember, however, although I have a few regrets in my life, this is not one of them. This should not be seen as a wish or a desire to have taken another, different path through life, other than the one I have lived. Rather, it is a remembrance of a time of innocence, long past, and of a time and a place that no longer exists, save for old photos and in my memory.

We both moved on from that time, that place and that relationship and we each found others to love and with whom to share our lives, but there is, and always will be, that time, that place, that sweet, young love, and that memory that I will always cherish. Kind of funny, I just realized that one of the songs I associate with Lynn is "Cherish" by the Association. That might be one of those Freudian things. Did I mention that she is beautiful?

Lynn met and married an Australian, and, quite naturally, moved to Australia with him, where they lived, had children, raised a family and created a life. Her children are successful, each in their chosen field, and she, in our periodic interactions, appears to be content with her life. I am happy for her, and continue to wish her every bit of happiness that she can find.

Lynn returns to the States every once in a while, and I have been lucky enough to have seen her perhaps 2 or 3 times over the past 50 years. A while back, perhaps 15 or 16 years ago, I was in California and met up with Lynn and Meri on one of Lynn's visits to the States. The three of us met for lunch in Huntington Beach and then walked on the beach together. We were three adult friends, friends since high school, visiting, catching up, sharing old memories and making new ones.

I lived in Spokane, Washington, but was staying at Meri's home in Burbank with Meri and her husband, Ken, during my visit. The three of us, Meri, Lynn and I, made arrangements to meet again in a couple of days, this time for a late lunch/early dinner on the Promenade in Santa Monica.

Meri and I drove to the Santa Monica Promenade at the agreed upon time in the early afternoon. Meri suddenly remembered another, prior obligation and at the last minute became unavailable for the dinner the three of us had planned! It was going to be just Lynn and me.

Meri ditched us, so Lynn and I had dinner in a small, obscure Italian Restaurant on the Santa Monica Promenade. We shared a meal, a couple glasses of wine and had an enjoyable evening stroll along the Promenade, sharing conversation and memories. We occasionally stopped to listen to street musicians and to watch street performers.

She is beautiful, still, and I can yet see the young girl I fell for so long ago within the woman she has become. I sometimes wonder...If things had worked out differently... But, life has worked out the way it was meant to be.

We each lived the life that we were supposed to live. We have each had our joys, and our sorrows. I would be strongly disinclined to trade the life that I have lived and enjoyed for any ethereal, unknowable, other life that might have been. Most of my life has been good, happy and filled with contentment. I would trade it for no other.

WESTMINISTER 1965-1971

My friends and I made it a point to attend our high school events. We went to football games, basketball games and the dances that followed most athletic events. We were simply normal teenagers in Southern California in the second half of the 1960s. Our lives revolved around family, school, friends, the beach, boyfriends and girlfriends, and other local attractions of that time and place.

In 1969/70, my junior year, Westminster High was a viable contender for league champion in several different sports. There was, of course, a cross-town rival, Anaheim High. It was widely believed that Anaheim could, and would, unseat Westminster, the prevailing champion for the past few years. And, indeed they did.

There seemed to be a themed dance nearly every month; The Homecoming dance, the Christmas Formal, and the Prom in the spring. We went to the Sadie Hawkins dance, and sock hops. Many a young romance blossomed and died at these dances.

There was always the "In Crowd". They always hung together, knew all of the new dance steps, and always had the newest fashions. As often as not, the In Crowd was composed of athletes and cheerleaders, the beautiful people. I fully recognize the stereotype. In that time, and in that place, however, it was the reality upon which the stereotype was built.

It was OK, for the most part; we understood the hierarchy. And, it really had little impact on how everyone else interacted. We all had our circles of friends. Some overlapped, and some did not.

In the second half of the 20th Century, there existed an entertainment venue in which one drove one's automobile to an expansive outdoor area containing a large, white screen upon which movies were projected. Cars parked in designated parking spaces, each on a slight incline, rising toward the screen. Each parking space had a speaker, attached to a pole by a long, thick wire. The speaker was designed to be hung in the car window, and provide the audio as the film was being played. This was the American Drive-In Movie Theatre. And, in that gilded age, we had some of the best movies ever!

In 1968, the movies to go see were 2001, A Space Odyssey, or the original Planet of the Apes. Also showing, Rosemary's Baby and Night of the Living Dead, one of the very first, and best, vampire movies. For humor, The Producers by Mel Brooks, or The Odd Couple with Jack Lemmon and Walter Matthau. '68 was also the year that gave us the Beatles in Yellow Submarine.

In '69, the movies to see were Easy Rider, Butch Cassidy and the Sundance Kid, and True Grit. Midnight Cowboy with Dustin Hoffman and Jon Voight, the first X-rated movie to win the Academy Award for Best Picture, was also released in 1969.

'69 also gave us one of my all time favorite movies, Support your Local Sheriff, starring James Garner and Walter Brennan. It is a funny movie, a very, very funny movie. Your girlfriend might want to see Chitty Chitty Bang Bang with Dick van Dyke. Your buddies just had to see Steve McQueen in Bullitt.

There were several Drive-in theatres within a matter of just a scant, few miles. The Hwy 39 Drive-In was where families went for the night's entertainment. Teenagers usually went to the Warner Drive-in, known as the notorious "Passion Pit". This is the place to take your date. It was, after all, only $1.00 per carload to get in. And, this was a time when this is where you went to be seen. The snack bar was where you showed off your new girl, or possibly, let everyone know that you had again taken up with an old flame.

If you asked a girl to the drive-in and she said, "Yes" to the Warner, you just knew you had a chance... for... something. But, when you took a date to the Warner, you also knew that some younger kid would sneak up on your car at the worst possible time, bang on the car door or on the trunk, and then run off laughing. They knew which cars to hit, the ones with the steamed up windows!

Once a girl had been startled by this a couple of times, it was nearly impossible to get her back in the mood for much of anything. There were a couple of nights when I could have, and would have if I had caught them, very cheerfully strangled some younger kids!

On warm, summer nights, a bunch of kids in multiple cars might all get together to go the movies. Often, the older kids could only go if they took their younger siblings. Not only was it free babysitting, but the parents just seemed to know that a younger brother and/or sister in the car at the drive-in could be a very effective form of birth control. On the other hand, however, there were a lot of kids running around.

Most Theatres had a playground up front by the screen, there to entertain the kids until the movie started and during intermission. The snack bar was usually in the middle of the theatre lot. You could get soft drinks, popcorn, candy, hot dogs and hamburgers. The guys would be in their bathroom, bragging about their prowess with the ladies. The girls in theirs, laughing as they shared stories about the romantic ineptitude of their boyfriends.

At that time, there were a lot of movies to choose from with G and PG ratings. Although there were R and X movies, they weren't nearly as prevalent as they are today. Movies may well have incorporated sex and violence in the story line, but these were not the primary focus. In the movies in today's world, it sometimes seems that the story is incidental, and the sex and violence take precedence. Then, such things were implied and suggested, but seldom shown. Today, it is unavoidable.

The intersection of Main Street and Pacific Coast Highway (PCH) was on the beach in Huntington Beach, less than 10 miles from our home. Huntington Beach was the Southern California, laid back community, known as Surf City USA. PCH was lined with surf shops, head shops and liquor stores, swim suit shops and cheap motels, most of which seeming to be on the perpetual verge of failure and bankruptcy.

It was also home to the Golden Bear, a small, contemporary music venue, where admission was only $5 to $10 to see such acts as BB King, Commander Cody, Steve Martin, Arlo Guthrie and others. The concert I remember at the Golden Bear was Tom Waits. They also featured Jimmie Hendrix, Joan Jett and the Blackhearts, the Chamber Brothers and Jerry Garcia. It was a VERY happenin' place.

On the beach were taco stands designed to look like thatched huts. This is where we bought hamburgers, hot dogs and soft drinks and rented surf riders and boogie boards. There were palm trees, open sand and pounding surf, but best of all, there were girls... in swimsuits... and bikinis! Not that we would know what to do with them if they ever noticed us, but we certainly could, and did, look!

You couldn't drive on the beach, but just a little ways north from Huntington Beach pier, was Tin Can Beach where you could park on the dirt shoulder of the highway. Once you parked, you walked to the beach past pumping oil wells, trying not to walk in puddles of oil that had leaked from the wells, and went on down to the pristine sands.

There were families that camped on the sand at Tin Can Beach for the entire summer. The husband/father would go to work; the family stayed and played on the beach. In the evening twilight, you could see men fishing in the surf. It was one way to help feed their families. For some families, depending on the distance to and from work, the father only made it home on weekends, or every four or five days for short visits before returning to the oil fields.

Some of those men working in the oil fields would work 12 hours on and 12 hours off with four and sometimes five-day weekends. The oil companies provided bunkhouses for the workers in the field, where men would sleep between shifts. Consequently, these men would only see and spend time with their family at those intervals.

There were also beachcombers on the beach at Tin Can. These were, for the most part, mostly men, and very few women. These were men who lived on the beach, often in shacks made of driftwood, or wood pilfered from local construction sites. Some would simply build a fire to warm the sand, move the fire over a couple of feet and snuggle down on recycled blankets into the warm sand where the fire had been.

Some made a living collecting and selling seashells and other flotsam that washed ashore. There were glass floats from Japanese fishnets, interesting pieces of driftwood and other treasures to be found. Because the beachcombers were few in number, the sea provided enough for each to scrape by on meager earnings made selling these treasures to tourists and seaside souvenir shops.

At the bluffs at the end of Goldenwest Street, where the street ends and the ocean begins, were beach parties, bonfires and music. It seemed that someone in every group always had a guitar, ukulele or bongo drums with them.

And, if a guy could find the "right girl", there might have been a certain amount of what we called "making out". There were also those occasional fistfights between teenage boys, but they never really seemed to be very serious. The weapon of choice tended to be fists, very seldom knives, never guns. We were, at a minimum, at least semi civilized. Those fights were, as often as not, over that "right girl" who just happened to be making out with the "wrong guy"!

The summer weather was warm and perfect, we were young, we were free, and we were truly blessed. We had the world in our laps and friends with whom to share it. Beach parties and bonfires were regular events.

If you could get to the beach, there were no other costs. If we had no other options, we could always hitchhike to the beach. At that time, hitch hiking was a reasonably safe form of transportation, at least to and from the beach. I'm pretty sure that hitchhiking got me to the beach more than any other form of transportation. As often as not, we would get picked up by other teens, also going to the beach.

Again, there were very few costs associated with going to the beach . . . unless of course, you wanted beach shack hamburgers, cheeseburgers, beach tacos or nachos, any one of which was only about 40 or 50 cents apiece, as I recall. A bottle of Coke or Pepsi was still only a dime.

There were times when, with a certain degree of subterfuge, you could get away with going up to a stranger's campfire on the beach, and help yourself to their hotdogs, chips and drinks. You watched for a kid about your size to leave the bonfire and go down to the water. You simply walked in, kept your face turned away or in shadow, and helped yourself to their groceries. If you acted like you belonged there, no one ever seemed to notice.

And, if you got caught, just run into the crowd! There were always a million or so other kids of the same size, shape, and age. They would never be able pick you out of the crowd! You know how those kids are. They all look alike!

Occasionally, wonderfully, spectacularly, the grunion would run. "What in the world is a grunion?" you ask. These small, slender, silvery fish have unique mating habits: when spawning season comes, typically in the summer, masses of grunion swim onto the sandy shores at night. The females dig nests with their tails and lay eggs. At the same time, the males come up on the sand to fertilize the eggs. Yeah, I know, in a manner of speaking, it kind of sounds like your normal, human teenagers.

The grunions' behaviors make them very easy to catch. There are thousands of them on the beach. Families flock to the beaches for the grunion runs. You take your bucket and grab as many of the wet, flopping, squirming fish as you can.

No fishing license required for those under 16, which makes it a great nighttime family activity. With that many fish on the beach, you can take as many as you wish, but it is asked that you only take what you can use. Wasting fish is unlawful in California.

Disneyland was close, about the same distance as the beach, just in the other direction. Disneyland, however, was reserved for special events. It wasn't something we did every day, but we did go.

The same was true with Knott's Berry Farm. It was there, and we went. Some of our friends and classmates were lucky enough to get summer jobs at these Southern California attractions. I didn't, I just wasn't that lucky! I worked at the McDonald's just down the street and around the corner from Westminster High School.

Minimum wage was $2.10 per hour, which is what we got paid at McD's. I put in around 20 hours per week, so was making about $45 a week with take home of about $35. Not bad when you consider you could take a date out for fast food and a movie for under $5.

Gas was $0.35 a gallon, so you could fill a 15-gallon gas tank for $5.25. I rode my little Honda motorcycle back and forth to work. It had a 3 gallon tank, and got about 45 miles to the gallon. I kind of wish I still had it.

At that time, nearly all of the workers at McDonalds were high school boys. Girls need not apply. There was no inside seating, although we did have a couple of concrete tables and benches outside on the front patio. All ordering and serving was done at the walk-up window.

We would call out our order as taken. "Taking 2 and one with one!" meant that we were taking 2 hamburgers, one order of fries and an apple pie. In this manner, the fry cook could keep up with the demand without too much waste. There were no smart terminals that showed on the cooks screen as the order was taken, it was all verbal. The front manager would tell the cook to "run 12, cheese 6" which meant fry 12 patties, and put cheese on 6 of them. If we had sufficient cheeseburgers the cook might ask "On 12?!?" – The response would be "All Meat".

Being teenage boys, we devised a similar code whereby we could alert our co-workers about customers worthy of note. Usually female customers. If a particularly cute girl came to the window, the call would go out, "All meat on Window 3!" If she was less attractive, but still passable, the call would be "Meat and Cheese on Window 2!" If not even passable by the standards of the day, the call would be "Nuttin' but Onion on Window 4!" We were teenage boys. Not bad kids, just insensitive . . . and heavily into puberty.

Knott's Berry Farm had no parking or admission charges then, preferring patrons to spend their money on food and souvenirs. If you wanted to go on the log ride, or the stagecoach, or ride the train and get held up by outlaws, you bought the ticket for that specific attraction.

A date at Knott's might cost as much as $10.00, so that was reserved for that special someone, de jur. In 1967, a chicken dinner at Mrs. Knott's Chicken Dinner Restaurant cost $2.75. Dinner consisted of salad, fried chicken, mashed potatoes, veggies, and biscuit, with coffee, tea or milk included in the price, as well as a slice of pie for dessert. You simply could not go wrong with a dinner date at Mrs. Knott's.

It was about this time when the cultural and social change in America began in earnest. Larger and larger segments of society were beginning to question the wisdom of our involvement in South Viet Nam.

The pacifist anti-war crowd and hippies began showing up almost everywhere, not just Greenwich Village, San Francisco and Berkley. Colleges and universities across the nation became incubators of political discontent and proponents of a complete rejection of the cultural status quo.

This was a part of the reason why Knott's Berry Farm found it necessary to put up a fence and begin charging admission. The hippies discovered that how easy is was to get into many of the buildings after hours. Multiple people, without permission, began spending their nights at Knott's, stealing from the stores and vandalizing the property.

The fence became a necessity. Charging admission kept out those who could not afford to pay. This, of course, included most of the hippies. This was the goal. Unfortunately, as an unintended consequence, young local families could no longer afford to take their kids to Knott's Berry Farm for a summer day's respite. What had once been a regular family event now had to be relegated to a status of only special occasions.

The 2nd American Revolution, begun in the 1960s, initiated substantial and significant change in our social and cultural landscape. Some of that change was beneficial, some was not. In many ways, that tumultuous period in American history set the stage, creating what it has now become, a place I no longer recognize as the country of my youth. America was once a place of God, families and patriotism. It no longer appears to be, at least not as it once was.

I'm not going to delve into the politics of that social turmoil, but will try to merely to describe it as I saw and experienced it. I do believe, that, in some instances, we may have discarded much that was good in America. I have seen our society become louder, cruder, ruder and much more disrespectful than it was when I was a youth. It truly saddens me.

America has never been a perfect place, but it was a place where, in my experience, people treated each other with respect, even when they disagreed. Cursing, denigration, cynicism and violence have, in many instances, replaced civil discourse. As Indira Ghandi said, "You cannot shake hands with a closed fist."

I am, to some degree, thankful that, at that time, I was blissfully unaware of much that was going on. I was only peripherally aware of civil rights marches and anti-war protests on college campuses. These events had no discernible effect on me.

As teenagers, we were self centered and self absorbed. We knew sport scores and rock bands, but most seemed to be almost universally disinterested in politics or political matters. That was something for adults. There were, of course, some in our cohort with political awareness, but, in the beginning at least, they were few, an anomaly.

There was to be, however, on October 15, 1969, a National Moratorium on the Viet Nam War. It was to be observed at Westminster High with a silent lunch hour on the lawn in front of the library. Of those students on campus who were politically aware, there were, of course, adherents on opposite ends of the political spectrum. We had a patriotic, anti-war contingent, as well as a cohort of patriotic, conservative students.

A rumor arose that the anti war crowd was going to take down the American flag on campus, so a group of student conservatives volunteered themselves to guard the flag pole during this event. The anti-war crowd planned nothing except to wear black armbands and have a silent, sit-in protest throughout the lunch hour. The Cons planned nothing except to protect the flag from a perceived threat.

Nothing happened. Campus was quieter than it had ever been during the school year. The anti-war crowd sat on the grass, and the Conservative students patrolled the flagpole. Political beliefs and affiliations were revealed and discovered. Friendships were made, cemented, and in some instances, discarded, based on one's political philosophies.

This event was in actuality, a catalyst that started many of us thinking about politics. Several of us were fast approaching draft age, and decisions made in Washington, DC would certainly have an effect on all of our lives.

We all knew of other Westminster graduates who were in the military, and some had been sent to Viet Nam. The ones who returned from Viet Nam were, in some indefinable manner, different. They were withdrawn, on edge, hyper alert, dangerous.

A CIVICS LESSON, 1967

THANKS MOM

While I claim that I was a fairly normal teenager for the times, my brother and sister were hippies. They wore the colorful, outrageous fashions and styles of the psychedelic hippy era, and participated in hippy events. They wore their hair long and went to concerts and could be occasionally found in Hollywood. They went to love-ins, Be-ins, happenings and Freak Shows.

They had their Hippy names. Even though I can never remember Celia's hippy name, Darrell's was "Plastic Man". His best friend and main partner in high crimes (emphasis on "high" crimes) and misdemeanors was a rather large fellow named Bruce. Standing several inches over 6' tall, 250 pounds and long, flowing locks of reddish, auburn hair. He drove a classic Jaguar convertible and was known as "The Red Baron", sometimes shortened to just "Baron". He was a regular at the house when Darrell came to visit. He was respectful to Mom and Dad, and they seemed to accept him.

On a warm fall evening, Baron, with my sister, Patty, on his lap, was reading bedtime stories. She was maybe 5 years old, and had, for some unknown reason, taken a liking to Baron, and he to her. He put her to bed, and he and Darrell went to meet up with Dad.

Dad was in a community meeting about 6 blocks from the house. Plastic Man and Baron drove over to the community center and pulled into the parking lot to wait for Dad. Darrell drove an old Austin that looked like an upside down, claw foot bathtub... without the claw feet. They were just sitting in the car in the parking lot, again, waiting for Dad.

They had been there but moments when 2 police cars pulled up behind them. The police ordered them out of the car, leaned them against the car, frisked them, and began taking car apart. They opened the trunk, the engine compartment and the glove compartment. They took out the seats and even pulled off the door panels!

During this sequence of events, the community meeting had adjourned, and several people stood around watching the scene unfold. Plastic and Baron sat on the curb, undisturbed. It had happened before, and it would happen again.

The police finally said, "OK, I guess you're clean. You can go." The police officers who take an oath to protect and serve didn't offer to put the car back together, they just left.

Dad hadn't really believed Darrell when he had previously said that they stopped by the police for no reason, other than looking like a hippy. He was beginning to question his prior convictions about law enforcement. Dad thought that if you got stopped by the police, you must have done something.

Occasionally, Plastic Man, Baron and their friends would go to tourist areas, simply to mess with tourists from other parts of the country. This was a time when it seemed that everyone wanted to visit California. California was the cutting edge place where everything was happening.

Tourists would pull out their cameras to take pictures of the hippies, so Plastic Man and Baron would take out their cameras and take pictures of the "Straights". For some reason, this always seemed to bother the tourists, as they would almost invariably duck or turn their heads away from the hippies' cameras. It was OK for them to take pictures of the local hippies without asking permission, but they certainly did not want their pictures taken by the hippies they were photographing.

One spring day, Plastic Man brought a young girl to the house, explaining to Mom that she was down on her luck, and needed a place to stay. She would be willing to help with housework in exchange for simple room and board, and her stay was to be for a just few days. They had a completely scripted story down pat and told upon arrival. But something about the tale just did not ring true to Mom.

Mom, a writer for the local newspaper, and sensing a story, began making phone calls to find out who this girl really was, what her true back-story might have been. Mom kept a stenographer's notebook next to the phone wherein she would record the date and time of each and every phone call, as well as take notes in reference to the content of the call. With each call she made about this girl, Mom left her contact information, name, address and phone number. She also kept that steno book record of the phone calls that she had made and with whom she had spoken.

Her calls about the young lady went smoothly in the beginning, but soon began to take on a rather strange, ominous character. At the start, people seemed to be very helpful in trying to help Mom help this girl, but after only a day or so, the people whom she called became very abrupt. She was puzzled, to say the least. The mystery deepened.

It didn't take very long before kids in the neighborhood discovered that there was an undercover police van parked down the block from our home with some kind of a listening device aimed at our house! Kids seem to notice everything that goes on in their neighborhood, but what in the world was going on, this time? Wow, undercover police surveillance and stuff?

Oblivious too much of this neighborhood police activity, Mom was attending Goldenwest College, taking classes in Writing, Poetry, and Music Composition. She was the driving force at Goldenwest to successfully initiate an annual Book of Poetry entitled, "Litera Scripta" to be written, edited and composed by students at the college and published annually. The first edition of this on-going series was dedicated to my Mom.

Anyway. There was a tangible, underlying feeling that something was happening behind the scenes, things we could not see. Something was coming to a conclusion. An eruption of some sort was imminent. There was nothing that you could put your finger on, but the feeling was pervasive. Plastic Man, as dense as he could sometimes be, was aware of the tension, but woefully incognizant of his own role in creating it. Once he figured it out, he made plans to take the girl and go somewhere, anywhere, but here!

I felt the undercurrent as well, and decided to skip school on that particular day. I watched much of the day's events unfold from across the street and from the homes of neighbors. As a young teenager, I was frightened for my Mom, and, at that time, learned to fear the police. I was also afraid that if I was recognized as part of that household, I might be arrested, too. What was happening was contrary to just about everything I had been taught about the police.

"If you are in trouble", I had been told, "find a police officer. They will always help you." The events of that day convinced me that what I had been taught was less than completely accurate. The police, it seemed, were not necessarily the ones to turn to in times of trouble. As a matter of fact, I had seen with my own eyes that they had the potential, the police power, the will and the ability to make things much worse than they had to be. Citizen's rights did not matter, unless the police decided that they mattered.

Again, some police agency had had a listening post, and had been monitoring our home for several days. They were fully aware of the relevant circumstances; that she and Darrell were no longer there. That didn't matter. They were going to continue doing whatever they wished to do. Mom's rights, they had decided, were irrelevant.

Mom had gone to class at Goldenwest at her normal, scheduled time, intending to go to class, run errands, and return home. It was going to be just another normal day in Southern California suburbia. She later remarked that, when she left to go to class, there appeared to be a lot of police activity in the neighborhood.

Later, Mom was told by her friends at the collage that the police had showed up just after she left and had been asking about her. Somehow, in a prime example of true government efficiency, they managed to show up at each successive location just after she had left. The police were obviously, unsuccessfully, trying to catch up with a little, middle aged housewife who kept outwitting them by going to the grocery store, the stationary store, the fabric store and the gas station.

Mom finally returned home, unloaded the car, and went inside. She had noticed while driving, both to the college and on the way home, that there were multiple police cars in close proximity to the house. She wondered what could possibly be going on.

Shortly thereafter, there came a knock on the door. A Westminster police officer stood in the doorway and began reading the Miranda rights card. He said, "You have the right to remain silent. Anything you say can and will be used against you in a court of law. You need not answer any questions without the presence of an attorney... "Mom cut him off and said, "OK, I'll wait for my attorney." She closed the door in the officer's face, locked it, and called Dad to tell him what was happening. She then went into the kitchen, made herself a cup of tea, went into the bathroom and closed and locked that door.

The police officers broke out a windowpane in our front door, reached in, unlocked the door and let themselves in. They briefly searched the entire house, determined where she was, and broke open the bathroom door. Mom was arrested, handcuffed and put in the police car!

Neighbors told us that they had seen police cars from multiple jurisdictions. We lived in Westminster, so there were a couple of Westminster Officers there, of course. It was simple professional courtesy. They were given the lead in the arrest, whether they wanted it or not.

And, as circumstances developed and the true story eventually revealed, it became abundantly clear that this was something that they, the Westminster Police Department, wanted nothing to do with or even be involved in, in any way, shape or form! Also present were police cars from the City of Orange and from the Santa Ana Police Department. Some cars were marked, and some were unmarked, but still, obviously, police cars. Westminster Police Department had been told that the girl was there, that she was being abused, and possibly being raped!

Obviously, none of this was true, and at least some of the agencies involved knew it wasn't true. The Westminster Police had been lied to by another Police agency, and they were NOT pleased. There were later reports that this whole sequence of events created extremely bad blood between and among various Police Departments in Southern California.

Our house was surrounded by a 6' tall, cinder block wall, as were most of the homes in our Southern California housing tract. The police, during the arrest, tried to climb the cinder block fence to secure the back of the house. The first officer to try was seriously out of shape, and physically unable to climb the wall, although I should give him credit for the effort.

The second officer to make the attempt was obviously younger and in better shape. This is a good thing, because as soon as he went over the wall, you could hear our beagle, Duke, baying and barking, informing the officer he was not welcome in our back yard. It looked if he had hit a trampoline on the inside of the fence, because he came back over the wall somewhat faster than he had gone over in the first place. He was decidedly NOT amused! The police decided that securing the rear of the residence was probably unnecessary.

The Westminster Police ran into a problem. They did not know Mom and she refused to confirm or deny her identify, so they were unsure of whom it was they had just arrested. She maintained her refusal to comply with their demands to identify herself, even to the point of being booked into jail as "Jane Doe".

While in county jail, Mom entertained herself by interviewing the female guards as though she were writing an article for the paper. She asked why they had become guards, what their family life was like, if the liked their job, their education, etc. And, there was no quit in Mom. The guards kept trying to question Mom and kept asking her questions. She merely answered their questions with questions of her own. Mom was not making many friends in the lockup!

Dad came home from work in Wilmington, called and retained an attorney to get Mom sprung from jail. The attorney finally advised Mom to cooperate at least enough that she could be processed and released.

It was later that we found out that the girl was the daughter of a ranking Santa Ana police officer, and that he was the one abusing her! She had run away from his abuse. The reason for the City of Orange Police presence was that they lived in City of Orange. Her father, knowing full well that she had run away, reported her to the Orange Police as having been abducted.

He had lied about Mom, his daughter, his own domestic situation and the actual relationship between them. This elaborate falsehood convinced Westminster Police to conduct the raid and the subsequent arrest. Our house had been under observation for a week and a half. The forces behind this fiasco knew she was not in the house, and that there had been no abuse what-so-ever during the short time that she was there.

Mom was tried in Orange County Superior Court on charges of Obstruction of Justice and Resisting Arrest. Up until the jury returned from their deliberations with a verdict, the District Attorney was trying to cut a deal in which all charges would be dropped. If Mom simply agreed not to sue the city for false arrest and unlawful confinement there would be no further legal action. Mom, of course, was too stubborn, and Dad was way too angry to do so.

In his instructions to the jury, the Judge told the jury that if they acquitted her, she would be in a position to sue, and they, the taxpayers on the jury, would have to pay any award she might receive through litigation. They found her guilty of Resisting Arrest to which Mom responded, "My husband has multiple guns in the bedroom. If I had been resisting arrest, the first son of a bitch forcing his way into my home would have been dead!"

Mom and Dad thought that attending and observing the trial would be a good lesson in the American system of Justice for me. I was excused from school for the duration of the week- long trial, and, yes, I learned a lot about how our system works. Case in point; the girl's father, a police officer, was allowed in the court room in full uniform, and carrying his service weapon in a holster. The starched uniform was worn in court, I believe, to bias the court. The service weapon, I believe, was carried in court to intimidate the defendant, her family, friends, supporters and witnesses.

This officer's actions and conduct had the intended, chilling, intimidating effect on me and on Darrell. I'm not sure how it affected Mom and Dad, but I can guarantee they were not pleased. One, and perhaps both of them, began referring to the proceedings as the Kangaroo Court. We, however, were not even allowed to have as much as a pocketknife.

If the Internet and social media had been available then, the outcome may have been much different. We simply didn't have access to the same resources that the government had. Additionally, this was a time when people gave a blind support to the police and government agencies. Most people thought that if you were arrested, you MUST have done something wrong. There was a lot less willingness to look at the actions of the police with any kind of a critical eye, or to question those actions. They did what they had to do to "protect and to serve".

Dad was disinclined to repair the front door window broken out by the police during Mom's arrest. Instead of replacing the glass that the police had broken, he fitted a small piece of paneling to the window opening, upon which he wrote the following; "For this beautiful addition to our home, we would like to thank the combined police departments of Westminster, Santa Ana and orange". That sign remained on our door for several years, until 1978 when Dad transferred to Denver and sold the house.

Public Enemy #1

TRANSITION – CIVILIAN TO SOLDIER

I had fallen behind at Saint Anthony's, in large part because I did not want to be there. I had decidedly not applied myself to my studies. On return to the public school system, I was ill prepared to catch up with my contemporaries. I looked like it was going to take two and a half years to complete the requirements of the next two years. I had already been held back once, in second grade, and I was not going to go through that humiliation again. I was not going to continue going to high school after my peers had graduated.

Therefore, after my junior year at Westminster, I dropped out of the formal school system. I took the GED tests and passed with flying colors. On the other hand, however, I didn't really drop out of school. I simply took a different path to the goal of graduating high school. In this manner, I graduated a year before my contemporaries.

I also completed four of the five College Level Exam Program (CLEP) tests and accrued college credit in several core areas such as Social Studies, English and basic Science. I failed the CLEP math test. It wasn't until much later that I came to the realization that Algebra is NOT, in and of itself, a mathematics class. It is a language class, the language of math.

I hung around for the next 6 or 7 months working for Robert Shaw Controls in a packaging warehouse in Huntington Beach. I decided to enlist in the Army. I didn't see a real future where I was, nor did my life have any direction. I submitted my resignation to Robert Shaw Controls, indicating that I was enlisting. If I survived my enlistment, the company was required to re-hire me when my enlistment was up.

I had a few days left before I went in, so I was planning to pick up my last paycheck and party. I wanted my last week as a civilian to be memorable. This I achieved, just not in the manner I would have preferred.

Feb 8, I was on my way to pick up my final paycheck and I saw a friend walking to school. I stopped and picked her up, the school was right on my way. I stopped at the convenience store across from the high school to drop her off. There were several police cars and officers at the store, but I had no idea why. I wasn't concerned, I had done nothing wrong.

I went inside and bought a soft drink, got in my car and started to pull out. A police officer stood in front of my car and ordered me to "Park it!" I did as instructed, put the car in park. The cop came over, opened the door, grabbed me by my jacket, and pulled me out of the car! He then slammed me against the police car with enough force that my knee dented the car! I had no inkling, no clue what was going on!

I was handcuffed and put into the back of a police car, along with two other guys. We were taken to the Westminster Police Station, where we were processed, fingerprinted, photographed, and allowed to make a phone call. I called Mom and told her as much as I knew about what was going on, which wasn't very much. She said she would come down and try to figure out what the issue was.

I had been picked up in the morning, around 7:30. I called Mom at about 10:45, and there was some sort of a hearing at 1:00 pm. I was formally charged with "Loitering". They spouted some sort of legalese nonsense, and told me I owed some amount of money to the city for their inconvenience in having had to arrest me for loitering.

Mom spoke up and asked the magistrate if she could get my signature releasing my paycheck to her, so the fine could be paid. He graciously allowed this. I signed, Mom left, and I went back to my jail cell, albeit very briefly.

As soon as I got back in my cell, I was taken out and put on a Sheriff's bus. The bus was touring Orange County, stopping at all of the municipal jails, picking up prisoners for transfer to Santa Ana's main jail. Mom kept trying to catch up, but always seemed to be just one or two stops behind me.

Someone finally told her that it would be easier to just wait for the bus to complete its rounds. I would be at the main jail and she would be able to pay the ransom, err, fine, and get me released. She was also told that that would be in the early evening. Mom went home to make supper and await Dad's arrival from work.

I finally arrived at the Main Jail, getting there at about 9:30 that night. I again went through in processing, and was put in a cell with another guy. Mom and Dad had been told that if they waited until midnight to bail me out, I would be credited with one day jail time which would reduce my fine by some, significant, amount.

No one told me anything. I had no idea about what was being done, or about anything else, for that matter. At midnight, Mom and Dad tried to pay my fine and get me out, but someone had lost my paperwork and they couldn't find me! Without the paperwork, I wasn't in jail. If I wasn't in jail, they surely couldn't let me out of jail. Keep in mind, this is 1971, there are no computerized systems, everything is on paper. If you don't have the correct piece of paper, nothing can be done!

Mom and Dad went back home with the intention of coming back in the morning. At this stage, all I was going to do was sleep, anyway, so might as well let Mom and Dad get some sleep, too. Dad was an early riser, and he expected to be back by 7:00 am on Feb 9.

I was awakened at about 6:00 in the morning by a strong earthquake! It was the 1971 Sylmar quake, registering a 6.5 quake on the Richter scale. I was at the door, yelling to get out, as were a lot of the other folks being held in the jail. It was insanely chaotic! The other young man in my cell was sitting on the floor with his knees pulled up, and very quietly crying. I'm not sure why, but his crying bothered me as much, or more than the earthquake.

I was at the door, yelling "Yo! YO! Get me out of here! Hey! Get me OUT OF HERE!" I would pause from time to time to kick out at that man that was crying and yell at him to "SHUT UP!" I could not stand it. I was on the razor's edge of a panic attack.

The quake finally subsided, and at about 7:30 that morning a jail guard came in and told me I was free to go. I went out and found Dad waiting. He said it had been a busy and interesting night: He had witnessed a lunar eclipse on the front lawn of the jail at midnight, experienced an earthquake at 6:00 in the morning, and had bailed his son out of jail at 7:00. Already a full day, and the sun was just barely up.

Two days later, on February 11, 1971, I raised my right hand and took an oath to "... protect and defend the Constitution of the United States against all enemies, foreign and domestic", thereby enlisting in the US Army. I completed Basic Training at Fort Ord, California, and then transferred to Fort Belvoir, Virginia, to be trained as a 62B20, Engineer Equipment Repairman.

Why I chose this specialty I will never understand. This was definitely not one of my better judgment calls. I am not a mechanic. I have never been a mechanic. I will never be a mechanic. This is not where my skill set lies. Actually, a pretty bad choice, overall, although there were some pretty substantial rewards reaped from that particular bad choice. I do OK in the theory of internal combustion engines, but when it comes to practical application? It just ain't happenin'!

1971 was an interesting year in America, and, I guess, in the world. The US was involved in the war in Viet Nam, the Cold War was a cold, harsh reality, and our culture was in the middle of a rapidly evolving transformation. We were transitioning from Father Knows Best and Ozzie and Harriet to Ozzie Osbourne and Who The Heck Is the Father? There were still folks around from the Beat Generation, and the Hippies, too, had begun making their mark in the annals of American history.

It was a strange period, that time between Rock N' Roll and Disco, from jeans, cotton t-shirts and tennis shoes to polyester shirts and platforms shoes. The peace and love, flower power generation were to some degree, losing those Marxist utopian ideals that they had so recently espoused. And in the process, they were losing themselves in the hard drug culture that followed. Many others in the counterculture matured and grew into adults. They finished their college educations, got jobs, had families to support and became a part of that establishment against which they had so recently railed.

Dad had taken me to the Los Angeles Armed Forces Induction Center and dropped me off at about 5:00 AM. We shook hands, he drove off, and I turned to the first page of a new chapter in my life.

I discovered that we were to be delayed in our departure to Ft Ord CA, so I called Mom at about 9:00 am, and she agreed to drive up to the LA Induction Center to meet me for lunch. She showed up just a few minutes before we were all to be sworn in. I could tell that she was proud of me as I raised my right hand and took the oath to "... serve, protect and defend the Constitution of the United States, against all enemies, foreign and domestic..."

When the Swearing In Ceremony had concluded, the NCO in charge said, "OK, whoever belongs to the visitor is dismissed for now. Be back at 1400 hours." Mom, from the back of the room said, "I guess he no longer belongs to me, he's all yours, now." She later penned the following verse:

I'm sorry I said he's all your own,

Really, I meant he's just a loan

He's yours, Dear Army for 3 years or more,

All yours to teach and train

But, please, dear Army don't send him to war

I want him back again!

Mom and I shared lunch at a nearby café and returned to the induction center soon thereafter. I cannot remember any of the details of the lunch, the menu, the drinks, nothing. Mom took a couple pictures of me in my cowboy hat in front of the Military Induction Center.

I went inside, Mom went back to her car for the drive home, and later, I was herded onto the bus to take us to Fort Ord for Basic Training. We arrived at Fort Ord late that night, were assigned to transient barracks, went to sleep and woke up in a strange, seemingly hostile, new world.

Pete — Induction Center 2/11/1971

Pete – Induction Center 2/11/1971

FORT ORD, CA - BASIC TRAINING

Fort Ord is a beautiful piece of property on California's Monterey Peninsula. I firmly believe that God specifically designed this part of the planet to test the physical capabilities of any human foolish enough to accept the challenge. A two-mile run? Not a problem. How about a two mile run, in dry, loose sand? Would you like to try PT exercises in that same, loose sand? Through chaparral and weeds, up and down sand dunes, we were run, we soldiers – in – training.

It was difficult and exhausting, but became less so with each passing week. Mission accomplished, goals achieved, boys turned into men, civilians turned into soldiers. Or, at the least, it was a journey upon which the first steps had been taken; from boy to man, child to adult, civilian to soldier.

Army Basic Training is one of the most physically challenging periods of my life. I learned a lot about myself, and about what I could do. I also discarded self-imposed limitations I no longer seemed to need.

Basic Training lasted for 8 weeks. The transformation of young human beings in this short period of time was incredible to behold; military haircuts, everyone wearing the same clothes, and maintaining the same rigorous schedule. We all shared 2 common adversaries, Drill Sergeants and the clock.

46 years later, I still remember his name; Drill Sergeant Aho. He wasn't as bad as some, and was, in actuality, better than most. He was hard on us, as were they all, but he was mostly fair. I don't remember him singling out any one individual for his particular attention. He seemed to make it a point not to pick the same target two days in a row.

Some of the other Drill Sergeants would pick one unfortunate soul and would make an example of him for the entire 8-week duration of Basic Training. It was not a pretty sight.

Other Drill Sergeants would provoke fights among the basic trainees, often as a way to judge the mettle of the men. Whereas some were willing to fight, others were more diplomatic, and others still would practice avoidance. Few of the confrontations actually came to blows, and those that did were promptly halted. Some hand-to-hand combat instruction turned into grudge matches, when built up enmity was unleashed. As Drill Sergeants said, "Good trainin', men, good trainin'!"

February 1971, I was 18 years old and in the United States Army, and in Basic Training. There were draftees and enlistees, Regular Army, National Guard and Reservists. Neither of these last two were considered by Regular Army to be real soldiers. They were just mere, simple-minded, weekend warriors.

We all went through the same training, but there were subtle differences. The draftees seemed to be less enthusiastic about the whole process and the Drill Sergeants noticed. We Regular Army soldiers appreciated the draftees for giving the Regular Army Drill Sergeant's a different, easier target upon whom to heap abuse.

There is a certain monotony that overtakes a person in these circumstances. You know that today is not going to be a good day, and tomorrow ain't lookin' too good either. You know that you are going to get up early, do lots of stuff you don't want to do during the day, and there are going to be some folks yelling at you, pretty much all day long. You knew, in the depths of your being, that it would not last forever. Strangely enough, upon completion of US Army Basic Training, there was a tremendous sense of pride and accomplishment.

There is one event that still stands out from the monotony of Basic Training. As I have said earlier, this was a period of civil and social unrest in our country. The counter culture was in full swing. Although there were peaceful "flower power" protests, there were also anarchists, even then, advocating the violent overthrow of the American government and the American way of life. One of these anarchist groups decided to pay us a visit at Fort Ord.

We were being trucked out to the rifle range in "cattle trucks". When we arrived, it was discovered that the range NCO had been assaulted, beaten and bloodied. Several M-16 rifles had been stolen, along with some quantity of ammunition.

Since we were first on site, it was decided that we should begin the pursuit of these villains. Each trainee was each issued 3 rounds of live ammunition and sent out into the chaparral on a skirmish line to try to locate the "bad guys". The idea was to simply saturate the surrounding area with GIs in order to locate the miscreants. The bad guys were, indeed, eventually located and taken into custody. For a while, however, it was as though we were already in combat, cautiously seeking armed enemies in rugged terrain. We know they had M16s, they had stolen them from us!

After the first couple of weeks, Basic Training wasn't really that bad. We were young men in the prime of our young lives. We ranged in age from 17 to 24 or 25 years old, with a few just a bit older than that.

The physical training and conditioning was designed to get the maximum result in the relatively short, 8-week time frame allotted for Basic. Very seldom did we walk anywhere. We were required to run almost everywhere we went. We had PT exercises several times a day. Drill Sergeants continuously told us how much fun we were having, that we were enjoying it and having a good time. There were occasions when I sincerely doubted their truthfulness as well as their sincerity.

We also had classroom work. We were educated in the General Orders, Military ranks and Military courtesy. We were taught Military history and Army traditions. We had classes on the Geneva Convention and on the definitions of war crimes. They gave instruction on and showed movies of the Nuremberg War Crimes Trials of Nazis after World War II. We were taught the difference between lawful and unlawful orders, and when we might be required to disobey our superior officers and NCOs.

There were long marches and bivouacs, small arms training with carbines and grenades. We ate well, albeit quickly. We were subjected to medical and dental exams and repairs. We had our eyes examined and glasses issued. We were given vaccines against every disease ever known to man, and for some that had not yet even been discovered! As Arlo Guthrie put it, "We were inspected, injected, detected, neglected and selected!"

We also had some, very limited, free time, usually on Sundays, but occasionally weekday evenings. There was a Day Room with a pool table, a ping-pong table, newspapers and magazines. They also had a vending machine dispensing cans of beer! Federal drinking age, including military bases, is, or at least was at the time, 18 years old. Of course, the beer was only 3.2% alcohol.

There were several men who simply washed out. During the Viet Nam era, the Army, Navy, Marines and Air Force all needed warm, breathing bodies. More men were being drafted every day. Under those circumstances, you had to be pretty pathetic, psychotic or sociopathic to wash out of basic.

For those of us who did complete Basic and graduated, there was, and remains to this day, a sense of accomplishment. Basic was no simple task, and it took fortitude and determination to complete, but we had done so. We earned well-deserved pride in our accomplishment.

Mom and Dad drove up from Southern California, and Mom's friend, Margie came down from Mill Valley to watch me graduate Basic Training.

Looking back at the pictures from that time, I certainly stood tall and straight.

After Basic Training and a short leave, I was on my way to Ft. Belvoir, Virginia, about 15 miles from Washington, D.C.

Pvt. Peter D. Canfield – Fort Ord, CA February 1971

Kids, Mom, Margie, and Pete – After Basic Graduation

WASHINGTON DC, MAY DAY 1971

I arrived in one of the DC airports on April 29, 1971, although I can no longer recall which airport. I took a bus to downtown Washington, and walked into a chaotic and unfamiliar world.

Mayday 1971 was to be one of the largest anti-Viet Nam War peace protests ever experienced. People were coming from all over the US, as well as anti-war and peace activists from other countries around the world. The streets were crowded with a steadily moving sea of humanity of every size, shape and description.

There were obvious government and business people in suits and ties, carrying briefcases, and ladies in dresses. I saw Hippies, protesters and Police everywhere, with Army jeeps parked just off of the main arterials. Police and Sherriff's busses passed in every direction. RFK Stadium was being readied for use as a holding facility in the event of mass arrests.

Loud music spilled from live bands, AM radios and 8 track tape players, each competing for attention. Live bands played anti-war protest songs from flat bed trailers. Drum circles maintained a subliminal beat to everything. Hare Krishna's were chanting, dancing and shaking and rattling tambourines. It was an absolutely insane sensory overload. Southern California's middle class suburbia, beach bum, surfer dude culture, had seriously failed to prepare me for any of this!

I spent the night in someone's Step Van. I had no clue as to whom it belonged to, but someone outside told me I could crash in it. I did so, but only dozed and briefly slept, although very lightly. Sometime in the middle of the night, a couple came into the van, and I could hear them whispering about who I might be. One of them mentioned my military "low quarter" shoes. The other said to just let me sleep, as I wasn't hurting anyone or anything. They then proceeded to engage in a rather physical, and audible, demonstration of their mutual attraction and affection. I rather wished they had kicked me out.

Morning came early, sort of. Although I dozed off and on, I never did really get to sleep. The couple continued making love, with full sound effects until around sometime around 4:00 in the morning. When it seemed they had finally fallen asleep, I quietly exited the van and resumed the exploration I had begun the day before.

Although activist and protester activity had slowed down through the night, it had never really stopped. There had been continuous foot and vehicle traffic all night long. If you listened just a little, you could easily hear people planning and plotting the events of the day to come in our nation's capitol. Some were serious, some trivial, but all were meant to disrupt. It was easy to ignore the normal voices, but not the whispers. For some reason, whispers demand attention and cannot be ignored.

A beautiful sunrise next to Washington Monument thoroughly and artistically illuminated the naked people splashing around in the Reflecting Pool between Lincoln Memorial and Washington Monument. It was obviously going to be a wonderful spring day. The cherry trees were still blooming, their sweet, pungent aroma competing with the equally pungent smell of marijuana wafting throughout our nation's capital.

I saw a young couple in a sleeping bag under a tree. Both with long, straight, hair, hers blonde, his, dark, obviously Hippies. It was also obvious what they were engaging in . . . an overt rhythmic, physical demonstration of their affection, each for the other.

A Park Policeman on horseback galloped up, reared his horse, and yelled "No f***ing in the Park!" The horse came back down on all four hooves and they galloped off.

I spent a day or so walking around gawking like a rube in the big city. And, that is just what I was. It was unlike anything I had ever seen or experienced. There were immense granite palaces of government, large monuments and sacred, secular temples dedicated to the wisdom of the past, and to those who had possessed that wisdom.

I, however, was not yet endowed with wisdom. I managed to have everything with me stolen. I had no extra clothing, no uniforms, no shave gear, nothing but what I was wearing, my cheap Kodak camera, and the little bit of money in my pocket. I had been distracted by... someone? ...something? ...for just a moment. When I turned back around, it was all gone!

There was nothing I could do but to return to the bus station and get to Ft Belvoir. I lost a lot, but learned a valuable lesson: Not all people are honest and/or trustworthy and there are times when life sucks, and there is nothing that you can do about it.

I arrived at Ft Belvoir reception station, told the Transient Barracks NCO at the desk of my dilemma. He looked at me like I was stupid, and rolled his eyes. He told that there was a closet in the back where they had fatigues and other uniform clothing that had been left by soldiers just passin' through.

I could take whatever I could find that fit me. I found some fatigue pants, a couple of shirts that didn't stink too badly, and an almost new pair of boots in my size. Only three pair of boots there and one pair in my size. Things were looking up. But, only just a little.

I found an empty bunk in the back of the barracks room behind a wall of lockers. I folded my newly acquired military clothes, put them in the closest locker, took off my civilian clothes and lay down on the bunk.

Just as my eyes closed, a junior NCO came into the room, turned on the overhead lights, and began yelling, "Everybody up! This ain't no summer camp! Drop yer cocks and grab yer socks! Get up! Get dressed! Form up outside in 10 minutes!"

Oh, great, I thought. Now what? There were only 2 options. First, do as I was told, and prepare to go outside and get into the formation. The other option, which I fully considered, was to try to sneak out a back door or window, hide and wait until everyone left, then return and get some sleep. I chickened out.

With my luck, they had already considered that option, and had stationed some NCO out back, waiting for me or--someone just like me to do just that. I got dressed in my charity fatigue uniform and stood the formation. We were told by the NCO in charge that there was some kind of civil disruption, and that we were going to downtown Washington DC.

We were issued web gear with all the crap that goes with it, canteen, bayonet with scabbard, ammo pouches, and first aid pouches. We were issued M14s, but no ammunition. I guess it was going to be all right if we stabbed someone with a bayonet, but we couldn't shoot them. I was OK with that. I didn't want to shoot anyone.

I wasn't very familiar with the M14, because I had trained with a M16. The M14 was being phased out. I guess that was OK, because without ammunition it was little more than a club, or maybe, with bayonet attached, a lance.

They loaded us up on busses and took us downtown. It was the middle of the night, so I'm not sure where we were, just that we were on a bridge. I didn't know DC well enough to pick out any landmarks, the only thing I really knew, was that I was pretty sure that I was somewhere.

To get into or out of Washington DC, it seemed that you have to cross a bridge at some point. The protesters' plan was to pull onto bridges and into major intersections with junk cars, jerk out the distributor cap and/or spark plug wires, and throw them into the river, or just take them and run away. The idea was to shut down all roads into DC, and by doing so, shut down the Federal government workers. I guess if they can't get to work, they can't cause mischief.

There were organized military units there, mostly MP, but the guys on the bus seemed to be in similar circumstances to mine, men from the transient barracks, just passing through. It seemed that they wanted every warm-blooded body they could find, not that they knew what to do with us once they had us there.

As the sun came up, more and more people began showing up. I saw a lot of police types who could never blend in, but I also saw them in deep conversation with other people who appeared to be Hippies, obviously informants. I witnessed money-changing hands from "Suits" to Hippies. I might have been naïve, but I really wasn't stupid. Some things were just what they seemed to be. We never really got organized, never deployed, just stood around near the busses and watched everything going on around us

We had protesters around us and in front of us, of course. They were everywhere. Although there were militants, vestiges of the Peace and Love Movement were well represented. There was plenty of "Flower Power". We had several attractive young girls come up and flash their breasts, asking if we wanted to go home with them. They would gently place flowers in our gun barrels while blowing pot smoke in our faces. The temptation was incredible! The oath I took said absolutely nothing about celibacy, and these beautiful girls were right there! Of course they were all beautiful, I was 18 years old!

We hadn't been there long when an Army officer arrived and seeing us milling around, asked what unit we were with. When we said didn't know, we were from the Processing Center Transient Barracks, the major asked the NCO in charge of us what the HELL he thought we were doing there.

There was a brief, private conversation between the recently arrived Major and the Sergeant who had brought us into town. Even though we could not hear the conversation, it was obvious that the Non-Com was not having a good day. The Major appeared to be instructing this NCO in the error in his ways, and asking him who gave him permission to think without appropriate supervision.

We were promptly loaded back on the busses and returned to Ft Belvoir, where we were told that we had never been to Washington DC, and that the events of the morning that we had just experienced, had never happened. Wow, then I must have been having some really strange dreams. What could have been in that cup of coffee the hippies had given me?

Around noon, I finally got to get some sleep. As they said, "Today is the first day of the rest of your life." Yes, it was, and yes, it is. We later learned that this was one of the largest protests of the entire Viet Nam Era. With over 7,000 arrests, RFK Stadium was turned into a holding facility.

Protesters were being brought in by the busload. Probably on the same buses that had taken us to town and back. Except that, obviously, it hadn't happened, we'd never been there. We know it didn't happen, because we had been notified by duly appointed and authorized authorities that it had not happened.

The next few days were days of chaos and confusion, but I was soon assigned to a training class, beginning the process of becoming an Engineer Equipment Repairman, 2nd Echelon. We were put into old, wooden clapboard, WWII barracks. They were all cold and drafty, but fortunately, it was a fairly warm spring, and we were moving into summer.

We got to know each other, young men from all over the country, most of whom, with few exceptions, had taken Basic Training in different parts of the country, and on different Army Posts. Over the course of our training, we formed friendships with other soldiers with whom we found common ground.

I was talking with a couple fellow GIs about gymnastics and tumbling, a sport I was interested in. Although never on a school team, I enjoyed that part of PE in high school, and actually became, if not adept, at least capable. I began showing off with handstands, walking on hands, doing handsprings and other simple tumbling routines.

It wasn't long before several other GIs were bouncing around the barracks, trying to imitate. We took mattresses off bunks and put them on the barracks floor, using them as gym mats. At a minimum, it broke the ice for several of us. We are lucky that that is all we broke! There was a lot of laughter shared and friendships made that day.

We attended classes in classrooms, and spent time in the Engineer School motor pool, applying the training we had just received. We also spent time learning how to operate the equipment we were working on. We had to know what it looked like, sounded like, felt like when it was working well. How else could we know if something was not operating properly?

The good news was that it was pretty much a normal workday. Formation at 07:00, breakfast from 07:00 to 08:00. At 08:00 we would form up and march over to the Engineer School, a short distance from the barracks. We would break for lunch around 11:30, and return for the afternoon session from 13:00 to 17:00. This was our Monday through Friday schedule. The rest of the time was ours.

Except, we were not allowed leave the Engineer School company area for the first couple of weeks. That consisted of several rows of barracks and the admin building that contained administrative offices, the day room, and the mess hall.

There was also, in the school area, a soldier's hang out called the Firebase Coffee House. They served coffee, tea and soft drinks, and provided newspapers and magazines from most major cities across the country. We had access to national magazines such as LIFE and the Saturday Evening Post as well as TIME, Newsweek, National Geographic and others.

Thankfully, our quarantine only lasted for a month. Finally, finally! We were allowed to leave the company area. Free at last, free at last, Praise the Lord, I'm free at last! We could go to the library, go to the Post Exchange, or pretty much wherever we wanted to go. Except, there were, of course, conditions. This was the Army, after all. We could leave our company area, but we could not leave Fort Belvoir. OK, the circumstances were not perfect, by any means, but they were better.

So, I was walking around Post with Butch. Butch was a Complete. Total. All-Encompassing. Southern. Redneck . . . from Mississippi. Deep, deep, deep in the woods, Mississippi. Down on the bayou, Mississippi. We don't cotton much to strangers, 'round here, Mississippi.

We weren't really friends as we had little in common. However, one thing we did have in common was that we were both in the Army, and we were both really tired of hanging around the company area and seeing the same, male, faces. We needed a change of venue and scenery. Neither of us really cared where we went, but we really wanted to go somewhere, anywhere that was not the company area.

We walked the post, as neither of us had actually seen it. We had each flown to DC, ridden the bus to the Fort, been delivered to the Company area, and there we had been since our arrival. We simply needed a change of scenery. We walked past Post Headquarters, colonial style brick buildings, with stately, white columns standing sentinel over expansive porches. There were beautiful, manicured parade grounds, with cannon and flagpole, exuding an aura of history and honor, of Southern Gentility. It was late spring, the weather was warm, the walks tree shaded, and the freedom to wander was priceless!

Butch and I had been to the Post Exchange, the restaurant where we bought real food and were circling back toward our barracks, not in any hurry, just drifting along. As we walked away from the center of the fort and Headquarters building, the clean-cut neatness declined. The road we followed had become less populated; there were more trees, seemingly planted at random, fewer buildings, and more space between them. Obviously still the fort, just more casual.

We came up to an intersection of the road we were on, and looking to the right, down a slight hill, we saw a couple of girls walking toward us. One of the benefits prior to the introduction of cell phones was phone booths. And, one was handy, right there on the corner. I stepped into the booth and pretended to make a call. In reality we were simply waiting for the girls to walk up to us. I turned to Butch and said, "I get the little blonde." That was when Phyllis came into my life, and I did get the little blonde. We met on that June day in 1971, and we were married in October 1974. That story, however, is for a future chapter.

In reflection, there is a rather ironic twist. Phyllis, "the little blonde", did not want to stop. She wanted nothing to do with two more GIs. She had been in the Army for over a year, and she had had her fill of romantically inclined soldiers.

Specifically, they were WACs, Women's Army Corps. Their military crest (insignia) was of Pallas Athena, a Greek warrior goddess. Phyllis' companion, Joyce, however, thought I was cute, and she wanted to stop and visit. Neither of them was interested in Butch. This is just an observation. It's not a judgment, just an observation.

As it turned out, they were on their way to the post library, but they had stopped to talk. We introduced ourselves all around and visited for a short while. Someone mentioned that the circus was on post. There was to be a performance that evening, so we made arrangements to go to the circus together. We went back to our barracks, and the ladies returned to theirs.

When we arrived at the WAC Shack (women's barracks) to escort them to the circus, a couple other WACs decided to join us. We already had one Joyce with us, but another Joyce joined us for the event, as did Butter. I never did discover her real name, but I am pretty sure that it was not "Butter." But, Butter she was, Butter she is, and Butter she will always be.

None of us had a car at that time, so, as a group, we all walked to the circus. Trust me, we were used to walking. I don't remember all of the particulars of the evening, except for one thing; while escorting them back to their barracks, just as we left the show, we got caught in a tremendous rainstorm! The sky opened up and just poured! In less than 20 steps, we were totally and completely drenched. We were also young enough to laugh and enjoy it. It made for a more memorable night.

As we returned the ladies to their barracks and the evening wound down, we made arrangements to meet up again. A few days later, on a Friday afternoon, I went to the WAC barracks to tell some of the girls about the Firebase Coffee House, and about the evening's scheduled performance, a duo who played acoustic guitars and sang folk songs.

There were a couple of other WACs in the barracks lobby. I didn't know them but I invited them to join us, as well. I must have been convincing, because word seemed to spread, and close to a dozen young ladies took me up on the offer. We were all headed to the Firebase!

As we walked over to The Coffee House, I purposely planned my route to go right past my barracks. Word had spread, as it sometimes does in close communities, and they knew I was coming. Someone said there might be GIRLS! The guys were there, of course. There were guys in the barracks area, guys sitting on the steps, guys leaning out first and second story windows.

There was a lot of good-natured whooping, hollering and catcalls going back and forth from both sides. We were all 18 and 19 years old, male and female, and for the most part, not quite civilized, at best, just barely housebroken.

WOW! I was so cool! Ok, I may have been strutting just a little, like I was somebody. And, there's a good chance that I might have been wearing a huge grin, as well. Most of the guys in the barracks had not been this close to any female girls in a very long time! All of a sudden, I knew girls, and they were attractive girls! I was a very popular guy!

I told my barracks mates where we were going, and several of them hurried off to clean up. I went on to the Firebase with the girls, and the guys showed up as quickly as they could, after getting themselves washed, shaved and combed. I was later told that this was one of the biggest, busiest nights the Fire Base had ever had.

Several more WACs showed up a little bit later. It was a really great night! The chemistry was excellent, the vibe totally right on. The entertainment was great; both the professionals on stage, and the social interactions of everyone discovering each other, cultivating new and promising friendships. We were young people in our late teens and early twenties, far from home, enjoying one another's company. The summer of 1971 could not have had a more auspicious beginning!

From that first night, several friendships developed, as did several romantic relationships. Most were short-term liaisons, but a few actually lasted beyond that time and place. I was with Phyllis, the first girl we had met, the "little blonde". Jim hooked up with Rachael, Dean with Butter. We had an Air Force Airman with us in the Engineer School known affectionately as Wing Nut. I don't remember if Wing Nut hooked up or not. He was a bit older, a little more mature than the rest of us.

When we were finally released from quarantine a week or so later, and allowed to leave Fort Belvoir, we began going to a lot of different places together. We visited the Smithsonian and Arlington National Cemetery, Georgetown, monuments and museums and the Pentagon. We toured George Washington's home at Mount Vernon, watched movies, dined in restaurants, drank and we danced. We travelled to and toured Fort Washington, Maryland, a Colonial era fort on the Potomac.

My memory isn't what it once was, but the guys I remember are, Dean, a funny guy that later in life became a Drill Sergeant at Ft Ord, where I, as my Drill Sergeants so often reminded me, had so enjoyed Basic Training.

Jim, from Colorado, is of Native American heritage. In other words, he was that crazy damned Indian that always said he wanted to scalp someone. Jim survived a tour of duty in Viet Nam without so much as a scratch, a blister or a callus. While riding his motorcycle in the Colorado Rockies near Nederland, he was run off the road and of a cliff. He was pretty busted up with broken bones and internal injuries, but he survived. Viet Nam he could handle, Colorado drivers, not so much.

There was Bob, 17 years old, ineligible to go to Viet Nam because of his tender age, and a child prodigy on the organ. He became friendly with the chaplain to gain access to the organ in the Chapel. The Chaplain liked him, and he played the Chapel organ for the Sunday services.

The Chaplain even loaned his car to Bob, a 1971 Fastback Mustang. This was not a good move. Somewhere along the line, while cruising in the Chaplain's Mustang, we picked up a US Marine who happened to be of sufficient age to buy alcohol. In this instance, it was probably Boone's Farm Apple wine, or maybe some Annie Green Springs.

We all started drinking as we drove around the post. The Marine also had a car. He took a couple of our guys with him so we weren't as crowded. He followed as Bob wound around Fort Belvoir. It eventually turned into a driving competition of follow the leader. First one, then the other would take the lead, and the other had to keep up.

I was in the Chaplain's car with Bob. We came around a sharp turn, driving way too fast, when we came to a stop sign. Bob stood on the brake and came to a ragged, screeching stop. The Marine in the following car did not. He slammed into the back of the Chaplain's Mustang! There was a flurry of activity, with guys piling out of both cars.

I was pretty drunk by this time, as were the rest of them. We were however, sober enough to know that we were in deep kimche'. I did the only intelligent thing I could: I fell down into the barrow ditch and passed out. The weeds closed their canopy above me.

The Military Police showed up, and pretty much everyone went to jail to get it all sorted out. They missed me, passed out in the ditch and hidden by the weeds. I woke up at about 3:30 in the morning. I was cold, I was wet from the runoff in the shallow ditch I lay in, and it felt like my head was ready to explode.

I spent several minutes puking up the cheap wine we had drunk. I spent several moments more sitting by the ditch and cussing! It took me a while to get my bearings, but figured it out and walked the 2 or 3 miles back to my barracks. I got in at about 6:30, just after sunrise, found my bunk, fell on it and went back to sleep. It was Sunday morning, and I could sleep. Thank you, Jesus. Thank you, Lord. I am ashamed to admit it now, but that was the most praying I had done in a very long time.

Add in Stretch, a kid nearly 6 ½ foot tall and skinny as a rail, from Inglewood, California, just scant blocks from Los Angeles Airport. He was so thin he had to stand in the same place at least twice, just to cast a shadow.

Stretch had an affinity for slow gin fizzes, and absolutely no tolerance for alcohol. He could get drunk just walking past a liquor store. Our class was rounded out by our two Southern Rednecks, Butch and Catfish.

There were others, of course, of all races and cultures. I am afraid I have forgotten many of the names over the ensuing years, but I remember the faces, I remember the men. I do know that many of my classmates from the Engineer School went to Viet Nam. I also know that several did not come back.

The time we spent together was actually pretty short, from the first of May to the end of August, a scant 4 months. A lot seemed to transpire over that short span of time. Our experiences through that time shaped us, created us. At that time, the average age of soldiers in the US Army was between 18 and 19 years old. Most of us were on our own for the first time, and we didn't really know as much as we thought we did. We had some learning to do, and we had some maturing to do.

The daily leadership positions rotated among the members of the class. Almost everyone was class leader for some short period of time. When Butch, our Mississippi red neck was class leader, I remember our platoon marching on a collision course with a platoon of South Vietnamese Soldiers.

Butch turned his head, looked over his shoulder at the platoon and yelled, "Guide around the Gooks!" This was definitely not the politically correct terminology with which to refer to our beloved allies.

Oh, Yeah. Catfish. Catfish was about the nicest fellow you could ever meet. And, one of the largest human beings I have ever seen. But, Catfish was just a bit slow. I once saw him take two full days to get a joke. When he did get it, he laughed for a full week. Seriously, it would take him two and ½ hours to watch 60 Minutes. He could, however, keep rhythm with the flat of his hand beating on his knee and chest. It was something to behold.

Our Platoon Sergeant, Staff Sergeant Whitehead, was a very soft-spoken black man. He had enlisted in the Army when he was 17, and was now in his 30s. He was assigned as our Platoon Sergeant, but we really didn't see him much, except at morning and evening formations.

We didn't know much about him, but thought him to be a bit slow, that he was just putting in his time until retirement. His name was Whitehead, but we, in the beginning, referred to him as Sergeant Pinhead. In the some military units, there is an adversarial relationship between the lower enlisted ranks and those on a 2nd or later enlistment and of higher enlisted rank. It is sometimes good-natured, but can occasionally be fairly toxic. We considered our teasing to be rough, but of a good-natured variety. A L I F E R was just that, a Lazy, Inefficient Foul-up Expecting Retirement

We were at morning formation when the command was given and repeated down through the ranks, "Attention to Orders!" We perked up, as this was something out of the ordinary. We saw that there were additional officers and more, higher ranking NCOs than was normal.

"Sergeant Whitehead, Report!" He marched to the front of the formation and briskly responded, "Sergeant Whitehead reporting as Ordered, Sir!"

A Sergeant Major began reading the citation regarding Sergeant Whitehead. "... displayed exceptional courage and fortitude... in the Republic of South Viet Nam, in that he did, with little or no regard for his own safety, repeatedly charge an enemy machine gun position, overrunning that position and... During... this battle, Sergeant Whitehead although wounded twice... continued his mission... dragged 2 wounded soldiers to safety... under intense enemy fire... Therefore, Sergeant Whitehead is hereby awarded the Silver Star." The Silver Star is the second highest medal awarded, just below the Congressional Medal of Honor. Never again did anyone refer to Sergeant Whitehead by anything other than "Sergeant Whitehead".

A major lesson was learned by many of us on prejudging people, and on the concept of respect as something not given, but something earned. We were sufficiently aware of our own actions to be ashamed of how we had treated him, and thereafter, made every effort to treat him with dignity, and with the respect that he had most certainly earned. Godspeed, Sergeant Whitehead, Godspeed. You made a positive impact on a young man, and I sincerely appreciate it. Thank you.

Not everyone developed the same relationships, nor did the relationships develop at the same speeds. I once borrowed Dean's car to take Joyce out on a date, and had to borrow gas money from Phyllis to do so.

Bob, the kid, took Phyllis to see the stage show "Hair", a seriously anti-war, stage production being presented in Washington DC. He thought taking her to the show entitled him to a physical return on his investment. She let him know, in simple, direct language that could not be misunderstood, that that was NOT a valid assumption.

Jim and Rachael had a fling, even though she was married. Her husband had been discharged from the Army and had returned to their home state of Oregon where he was awaiting her discharge.

As a group, we found an out of the way swimming hole, complete with rope swing. It was a truly good time for all of us. We were all in the Army, male and female. Most of us were single and a long way from home. We were young and there was an unmistakable energy in the air. This was no time to be standing still!

We had things to do, we had places to go, people to meet, and, just as a reminder, there was a war on. That one, small fact truly changed our perspective on everything. We knew that, within the next year, some of us would be sent to Viet Nam, and that some who went to Viet Nam would never return.

Actually, there were two wars happening at the same time. A violent, dirty war half a world away in Viet Nam and a social and cultural war right here at home. Colleges and universities were being taken over by students and protestors, and the Black Panthers were demanding racial justice. In the preceding decade, JFK, Bobby Kennedy and Martin Luther King had all been assassinated. Richard Nixon had been elected President of the United States in 1968, and would be again in 1972. The Watergate scandal had not yet occurred.

Our society was rapidly changing, with many traditional values rejected by the upcoming generations. Society could not change overnight, although there were times when it seemed to happen exceedingly fast. Some of us were politically aware, and some of us were still, in many regards, just kids, unaware and disinterested.

We were varied and changing groups of teenagers and young adults, all going to different places and different events. We went swimming, and to several of the Smithsonian Museums. We explored Washington DC, its grand buildings and monuments, and respectfully and reverently visited Arlington National Cemetery and the Tomb of the Unknowns. Experiencing Georgetown's nightlife and, quite simply, being young and unfettered, away from home and parents.

On a trip to tour the White House, President Nixon, noticing our uniforms, called us over, thanked us for our service, shook our hands. To me, he appeared drawn, tired and distracted. I was still in awe. I had just shaken the hand of the President of the United States. It was, and it remains, an honor.

In the midst of all of this, I received notification that Grandpa C had passed away. Grandpa C was born in 1874 and died 1971, a life of some 97 years. He lived through a span of America's history that I had only read about in schoolbooks and historical novels.

He rode horses before there were automobiles to be driven. He could drive, of course, both an automobile and a team of horses. Family legend has it that he drove his first car through the back wall of the barn while pulling back on the steering wheel as if they were reins, yelling "WHOA, You son of a Bitch, WHOA!!"

Grandpa was 26 years old when the 20th Century began, 55 years old on Black Friday when the stock market crashed and the Great Depression began. He was 67 in 1941 when American involvement in World War II began with the Japanese attack on Pearl Harbor. He was 95 years old when Man first set foot on the moon in 1969.

I requested, and was granted leave to go to Grandpa's funeral, even though it meant that I would have to be "re-cycled" into a later class to complete my training at the Army Engineer School. It would be worth it. I flew to Spokane, Washington where Dad picked me up at the airport for the ride out to the family farm.

The funeral was appropriately respectful and solemn. It seemed that the entire town turned out to pay their respects. The days passed quickly, and family members slowly returned to their respective homes. I flew back to Washington, DC, to Fort Belvoir, and to Phyllis.

Federal Troops – Washington DC Mayday 1971

Phyllis — circa 1971

Pete, Grandma C, Tony, and Patty – Grandpa's Funeral 1971

VIRGINIA STATE PEN

NOT YOUR NORMAL VACATION DESTINATION

Labor Day was fast approaching, and Phyllis and I decided to take a road trip. We would drive to Louisville, Kentucky, a distance of just over 600 miles, to visit my Aunt Nancy. We looked at the maps, and decided that we could make the trip, stay overnight with Nancy, and return to Fort Belvoir in plenty of time. We were mistaken. We were very mistaken.

We left on a Friday afternoon, and as night fell, we found ourselves on a two lane back road somewhere in West Virginia. We drove slowly through small pools of light from the one or two streetlights in each small hamlet and village. The villagers stared at us in every small town through which we passed. They seemed to watch our every move. We could feel the eyes staring at us.

On the other hand, once away from the towns, we wound our way through beautiful mountain and meadow byways with streams and brooks illuminated by the full moon. And we burned up our gas money. Very early Saturday morning, we did, finally, somehow, arrive at Aunt Nancy's.

The next day, we went to a "Frontier" re-enactment village, somewhere just over the Kentucky state line in Southern Indiana. We enjoyed period costumes and demonstrations of frontier skills such as blacksmithing and horseshoeing. I believe there was also a black powder, long rifle demonstration. It was a nice day, well spent getting re-acquainted with extended family. We went back to Nancy's and retired early, anticipating the next day's return trip to Fort Belvoir.

It would be a full day's drive back to Fort Belvoir, but we left early enough that we foresaw no problems. Our primary challenge being we didn't have enough gas money, and I was too proud to ask Nancy for help. I figured that if we couldn't get all the way, then we should get as far as possible, as fast as possible. It was the second part of that plan that I would later regret.

We were somewhere in southern Virginia when I got caught in a speed trap! The Virginia State Patrol was out in force on Labor Day. Although we were in Phyllis' car, a maroon 1966 Mercury, I was driving. The Troopers said I was going 85 in a 55 MPH zone. We were instructed to drive our car and follow the trooper's car to the Justice of the Peace. We arrived at the JP, and I was immediately convicted with little to no fuss at all. I don't think they even bothered to ask me much more than just my name.

It was simple, pay a $50 extortion, oops, I mean a fine, to the Justice of the Peace, and we could be on our way. The only problem being, I didn't have $50. I didn't have 50 cents. We had spent all the money we had on gas, and we still didn't have enough gas or money to get back to Fort Belvoir, and the side trip to the Justice of the Peace didn't help the situation.

Well, it was pay the fine or go to jail. I still didn't have $50. And, they really didn't have a jail. But, they did have the Virginia State Penitentiary. They put me in the Virginia State Pen--the Big House--for speeding.

OK, admittedly, I was not put into general population. I was in a separate holding area, in an individual cell. That didn't make it any better. I really did not want to be there, but there, indeed, I was. That part of Virginia has German Brown cockroaches almost big enough to put a saddle on and ride. At least when they handcuffed me for the ride from the Justice of the Peace to the State Pen, they handcuffed my hands in front. I still felt very intimidated driving up to the massive front gates of the prison.

I said my goodbyes to Phyllis and asked her to not leave me there for too long. I was taken away, and she was left standing there in the lobby of the Justice of the Peace's office. Phyllis didn't have enough gas and she had no more money.

She asked the State Troopers if they could help her out with a little gas money. Among the several officers, they raised almost a dollar for a 5 ft. tall, 100 pound, 19 year old girl, who was stranded about 175 miles from home. It was such a wonderful, generous display of that hospitality, charm and gentility in which so many Southern Gentlemen take pride. You know, that undying sense of chivalry all Southerners seem to claim.

She drove north, at exactly the speed limit, eventually stopping at a highway rest area where a truck driver gave her a couple dollars. That was almost enough to get her back to Fort Belvoir. She called an on-post friend to bring her a gas can with enough gas for the last few miles of the trek.

While she was managing to get back to Ft Belvoir, I was given my phone call. I called my First Sergeant and told him the story. He basically told me to get my ass out of jail and get back to post. And, do it NOW! Yeah, Top, I'm working on it.

Phyllis got the money together for my speeding fine, and prepared to send it Western Union to the County Justice Of The Peace. However--there is always a 'however' in these stories--she could not remember if the Justice of the Peace was in Mother Goose County or Crazy Quilt County. As it turned out, it was neither. Anyway, she sent the money... somewhere... and it simply disappeared. Never sent, never received.

Things were not going well. I was still in the cell in the pen. I did not want to be there. I was outnumbered by cockroaches, spiders, and other strange bugs and I really had nothing to do. I asked for paper and pen to write a letter to my parents. One of the guards brought me 4 sheets of penitentiary stationary and a pencil. I was told that prisoners were only allowed 4 pages at a time. All righty, then!

The front of the paper was the same color and consistency of the Big Chief tablets we used in kindergarten and first grade. The back of each page had a list of prohibited items and forbidden contraband. It listed visiting hours for the State Pen, who could visit and who was prohibited. There was a red watermark on each page: "CENSORED!"

I wrote a short, friendly note to Mom. "Dear Mom, the Army life is going OK I guess. Not too much to report from here. Phyllis and I had a nice drive to Kentucky, and a good visit with Nancy, etc." There was no indication as to why the prison stationary, no reason, no explanation of anything. Mom could have killed me if she had been close enough.

Fortunately, I got back to Fort Belvoir before she got the letter and I called home when I got there. It was important that I speak with her before she got the letter and make sure she doesn't follow up. Mom could be tenacious about things like that.

Phyllis showed up, having driven back down from Ft Belvoir with the money to pay the fine... again. She had sent the fine once through Western Union, but that money had disappeared into the ether. She paid the fine in cash, in person, and I was released. We returned to base.

A few days later, as I was picking her up at her office, she went into Major Alec's office to tell him that she was leaving for the day. As I stood outside his office door waiting for her, out of his line of sight and heard him ask her "How's your jailbird?" I poked my head into his office and said, "I'm doing fine, Sir. It's good to be back on base."

Shortly after my return to Fort Belvoir, I completed the Heavy Equipment Mechanic's class, received my diploma and orders to report to the 50th Engineer Company, United States Military Academy, West Point, NY. I took a couple weeks leave and flew home to Southern California. After my leave was up, I followed my orders and flew cross country from Los Angeles International Airport to New York City on my way to the United States Military Academy, West Point, New York.

While I was traveling, Mom was again writing:

The WAC that Pete thought was so cute would have thanked him

But the Army it seems has outflanked him

His request for a date

will just have to wait

The romance is doomed, she outranked him!

Thanks, Mom.

UNITED STATES MILITARY ACADEMY,
WEST POINT, NY

Upon arrival at Kennedy Airport I caught a shared- taxi with a couple other people, all headed for downtown New York City. About half way to the city, I realized that I had left the manila envelope with my orders and other military paperwork on the plane. I stopped the cab, paid my partial fare, and caught another taxi back to the terminal. I ran back to the airline gate. There was no TSA, no airport security screenings. At that time, there was no need.

Fortunately, my paperwork was still at the Gate where I had arrived, having been found by the cleaning crew who were cleaning and preparing the plane for the next flight. I got what I needed, and went looking for a ride into the city. Again. I have got to stop spending money on taxicabs to nowhere!

I thought I'd get a pack of cigarettes, but when I went to the concession stand in the airport, they wanted $7.00 a pack! This was in 1971, when cigarettes were about $.50 a pack in liquor stores. You could buy a carton for under $4.00. In 2010, when I was still smoking tobacco, you could buy a pack of cigarettes for $5.00. I decided to wait on that particular purchase. I was running out of money, and still had to get from New York City to West Point, some 50 miles up the Hudson River.

I arrived at Grand Central Station in a cab, and then spent several eternities looking for the bus terminal. I knew there was a bus, because my orders to West Point had included an information sheet, and it said there were busses. I figured if the Army said there were busses, then there had to be busses. I just had not been looking where the busses were. OK, finally, I found the bus terminal, and eventually, a bus that would take me up the Hudson to Highland Falls and West Point.

I arrived at West Point in early fall 1971. I had turned 19 years old a month ago. I got off the bus at the West Point Visitor Center, located just inside the main gate. I asked for and was given direction to my Company. I walked the short distance up a slight hill to the 50th Engineer Company. The Engineer Company's mission was to provide the necessary support to the United States Military Academy, in alignment with our role as Engineers.

In other words, our job was to keep the roads plowed in the winter and swept in the summer. The current mission was to build new, electronic rifle ranges for the West Point Cadets, with targets that would "fall" when shot.

Building these ranges, we used pneumatic drills to drill holes into solid rock. We then load the holes with dynamite. The work was such that we would drill in the morning, pack the dynamite, blast at noon, eat lunch while the powder smoke cleared, and dig out the trenches after lunch. We would repeat the process in the afternoon, blasting again just before we quit for the day, and dig them out on the following day.

After digging the residue out of the trenches, electrical cable was laid, providing power to operate the targets. Other men operated heavy equipment such as bulldozers, to build berms, and road graders to level and grade access and parking areas.

We were trained to be "Volunteer" firemen, although it was not as if we really, actually, volunteered. It was more like we were being volunteered. I don't remember being called out to fires more than a couple of times, and those calls turned out to be minor events. The area around West Point is heavily wooded, so it made sense to have personnel trained in that discipline. There is actually much to learn in combating fire in rugged, forested areas.

When I arrived at the company, and reported in, the Company Clerk took my personnel file and glanced through it. Something caught his eye, and he showed it to First Sergeant. The First Sergeant showed it to the XO, and XO showed it to the Company Commander. Now I was concerned!

The CO looked at me for what seemed a very long time. Finally, he asks me if I would like to work inside the building. I thought that sounded like good idea, so I agreed. He then told me I was going to be assigned to the Mess Hall as the Clerk. Cool! Inside work, and free food!

Since part of my job would be to order and pick up food every week, I would have to get a military driver's license. I figured no sweat, I know how to drive, been doing it for years. Except of course, the Army can make anything difficult. And, they did.

I would be driving a deuce- and- a- half, so I had to qualify in a sedan, a jeep, a 5-quarter ton truck, a 5-ton, and a 10-ton lowboy. I was tested on pretty much everything except a deuce-and-a-a-half. I guess they figured that if I could drive everything else, I might be able to drive the deuce-and-a-half.

It is The Army Way. And, for future reference, there are only two ways of doing things: The Army Way, and the wrong way.

This wasn't a bad situation. A war was going on, but not where I was. That suited me just fine. Where I was, was upstate New York, some 50 or 60 miles up the Hudson River from New York City. It took about an hour and a half to get to Grand Central Station, and from there, the world!

I would go to the USO and get free tickets to Broadway shows, as well as some off-Broadway shows. I also saw some shows that were way off – off – off Broadway. I saw a Gilbert and Sullivan festival at the Light Opera of Manhattan, with very well done presentations of Iolanthe and HMS Pinafore. There were a couple of other shows I saw, but these 2 stood out.

I maintained contact with Phyllis, although that required a certain amount of coordination and persistence. Phyllis had access to a house phone in the E-5 Barracks, where she lived, and I had a bank of phone booths on the ground floor of my barracks, with two phones on each side. There were also about 150 guys living and working there who also wanted to use the phones.

There were no cell phones and no personal computers. Computers were something found primarily in Science fiction books and in movies. And the closest thing to a cell phone was Dick Tracy's wrist radio.

Getting onto the phone could be a real challenge, and usually involved waiting in line, but we managed to talk once or twice a week. It just took a whole bunch of dimes. On a good day, usually on weekends, we might get to talk for a full fifteen minutes!

In a rather strange twist, another fellow stationed at West Point with me asked if I had ever lived in Rock Springs, Wyoming. I was startled, but responded "Yes, when I was in elementary school". It turns out that he was a neighbor in the trailer park across the highway from our house. Recognition finally struck me, and I asked if his name wasn't Jim, and he answered "Yes". Cool!

Jim knew of an available apartment above a pizza parlor, and asked if I would be interested in being a roommate. I thought about it rather quickly, and agreed that it would be good to have a place to get away to.

There was an additional benefit to this apartment. When they had left over pizza at the end of the day, we could get it very cheaply, sometimes for free. So, we ate pizza; Pizza for supper in the evenings, cold pizza for breakfast. And on Saturdays, cold pizza for breakfast washed down with cold beer. Could life even get any better?

Believe it or not, eventually, everyone gets tired of pizza, everyone. After I moved on from West Point it was several years before I could even contemplate ordering a pizza. Pizza was not the only thing we ate. We also had a pot of forever soup.

There was a pot left on the back burner that had a little bit of everything in it. Everyone was welcome to a cup or bowl of soup. The only requirement was that you put an equal amount of something in the pot. Take a bowl of soup, put in a can of green beans. Take a bowl of soup, put in a cut up loaf of Spam. Take some soup, put in a can of Hormel chili. Take some soup, put in something. We kept it going for 3 or 4 months, and it was actually pretty good! At least, I don't think it killed either one of us.

MERRY CHRISTMAS

December 1971, I was 19 years old, an E-3, Private First Class, in the US Army, making about $180 a month. I had free room and board, free medical and dental, furnished uniforms, and 30 days paid vacation every year. Of course, I also had the potential of being sent to Viet Nam and getting shot at. That was really not something that I wanted to do.

I had enlisted in the Army in February, completed Basic Training at Fort Ord California and AIT as a Heavy Equipment Mechanic at Fort Belvoir, Virginia. I was now stationed with the 50th Engineer Company, United States Military Academy, West Point, New York.

Although I was ostensibly a second echelon, heavy equipment maintenance mechanic, properly trained by the United States Army, I was probably the single worst mechanic in the Army. However, in a massive stroke of good fortune, I was assigned by the Commanding Officer as the Company Mess Clerk, working in the Mess Hall.

My duties consisted of maintaining the menu, ordering supplies, and driving either a 5/4-ton pickup or a 2-½ ton (a deuce n' a half) truck to pick up supplies at the commissary. I also supervised soldiers assigned to KP (Kitchen Patrol), a disliked duty, often assigned as punishment for minor infractions. However, my duty was fairly easy. I didn't have to go out into the upstate New York winters to work. For the most part, I got to remain in the warm Mess Hall.

With Christmas approaching, I had requested and been granted leave. I made plans to fly home to Southern California to spend the holiday with family, and had purchased my round trip airline ticket. My boss, the Mess Sergeant, told me that he would let me leave a couple hours early. He knew that I still had to take a bus to Grand Central Station, and then another to Kennedy Airport.

141

He assured me that he would sign me out on leave in the Company Log Book. I took off as soon as I could, took the bus to New York City, then the bus to Kennedy Airport, and flew home to Southern California. That pretty much used up what little money I had.

I got home on December 19, and visited with family and friends. Two days later, on December 21, my First Sergeant called me at my parent's home and told me I was not signed out, and that I must return. I protested, but to no avail. I had to return, or I would be AWOL, and subject to arrest by both Military and civilian police, which was not how I wanted to spend Christmas. I gave up, contacted the airline, and they allowed me to use my return flight early. I flew back across the country, took the bus from the airport, back through Grand Central, and returned to West Point. I signed my name in the company log, and was free to go. I was now, officially, on leave.

I decided to sleep the night in the barracks, as I really had no other place to go. But I certainly did NOT want to stay there! As I have written in earlier segments, while stationed at Fort Belvoir, I had met Phyllis, and we had hit it off quite well. Our first date had been to the circus, and we got caught in a massive rainstorm on our way back to barracks. That had been our first date and quite a few more had followed that first one. I have to admit, I was some smitten.

She and I had called and corresponded pretty steadily since I had transferred to West Point. Our relationship was well on the way to developing into something of much greater significance.

I called Phyllis, still at the Institute for Special Studies, Combat Development Command, Ft. Belvoir. She told me that friends, also in the Army, were letting her use their apartment in Woodbridge, Virginia while they were out of town over the holidays.

She invited me to come to DC for a Christmas visit. "Of course I'll come down", I said. "I'll get there as soon as I can." I had no money left, but I really did not care, I was not going to let that be an issue, and it did not deter me. I was NOT staying there in the barracks for Christmas! I simply wasn't going to stay there.

Early the next morning, I walked out the gates of the Point, and stuck out my thumb and began hitchhiking toward New York City. I'd been travelling since the previous morning's drive from home in Westminster to LAX, then flying across the country and riding the bus from Kennedy to Grand Central Station and on to West Point. In the past few days I had travelled over 6000 miles. There were only 300 more miles to go. As we used to say, "It ain't no thang!"

I soon caught a ride almost to New York City, actually right to the New Jersey Turnpike onramp. Perfect! There was simply no better place for me to have been dropped off.

Cold was the day with the weather worsening. Snow there was and hail, freezing rain and freezing fog, but I was not going back. I caught my second ride in just a few minutes. It was the Season, I guess. Or perhaps, I was just a pitiable sight, standing so forlornly in the rain and snow, shivering in the cold.

Remember also, this was a time when hitchhiking was actually a valid form of travel. I was a young man in my prime, a soldier, and I held no fear of strangers. It is a great misfortune that this form of transportation has been taken from other young people by evil predators.

Down through New Jersey and Pennsylvania to Baltimore, Maryland I travelled with my second ride. Not only did this fellow give me a ride, but when he stopped to let me out, he wished me a merry Christmas and gave me a five-dollar bill. I was very grateful for his kindness. I needed it.

With one more ride, again, quickly caught, I made it to the Capitol Beltway. The driver let me out in a restaurant parking lot. I went inside and called Phyllis from the payphone. She knew the restaurant, and drove out to pick me up, arriving in about 45 minutes. I spent $.50 on a cup of coffee and waited for her. It had taken me 3 rides and about seven hours for the entire trip, West Point to Washington DC.

We spent the afternoon and evening in the borrowed apartment, enjoyed a simple meal, then retired for the night, she in the bed, and me on the couch. The following day was Christmas Eve.

On every military base, there are always some who, because of duty or for other, personal reasons, do not go home for the holidays. There are always some who have no family or home to go to, the Army is their home and their family.

Phyllis and I spent the day visiting with friends, soldiers, who, each for their individual, personal reasons, were still in DC. During the course of the day, we met up with and visited others who hadn't much to do. By the time evening rolled around, we found ourselves in downtown Washington, DC very close to the White House.

We were several; military people all, from all over the United States and beyond. From the far West we came, from the Deep South and from the farthest Northern reaches of Alaska. From the Rocky Mountains and the distant Pacific shore, from the Plains, the prairies and the deserts, we all came together, equally sharing our loneliness, each with the other. Each of us committed to service to country. And, our loneliness, shared, was lessened. That memory is as vivid today as if it were yesterday, not 45 years ago.

We strolled across the moon lit, snow covered grounds, the night glowing, beautiful. There were Christmas trees from every state, each shining with lighted bulbs, glistening tinsel, baubles and a star upon each.

There was a live Nativity scene, with Mary, Joseph, Baby Jesus, shepherds and Angels.

In an enclosure were reindeer, wearing bells on their harness, with Santa nearby. Walking in the brilliant moonlight were couples holding hands and smiling. There were families with children, large and small. I was among friends and with a beautiful young woman who cared for me. It was a magical night.

There were Victorian Carolers, filling the night with music of the Season. We soon added our own voices, joining in, singing songs of Peace, Love and Joy, we Soldiers, we Warriors in that time of war.

As I said, I had little or no money, as I had spent what I had had going to California to spend the Holidays with family. It was a bittersweet irony when Phyllis gave me a wallet as a Christmas gift. I, unfortunately, had no gift for her, other than my presence.

The night waned, we said our good-byes to our companions and compatriots, and we each retreated to our own homes, whether Army barracks, mobile home or loaned apartment. Our first shared Christmas Day was serenely sweet. The day was filled with that quiet companionship that only a blossoming young love could have created.

The day after Christmas, Phyllis bought me a bus ticket to return to West Point so I wouldn't have to hitchhike. I was a lonely young man, far from home and family, and again, leaving someone about whom I cared. However, not really knowing it at that time, I was on the cusp of creating, with her, our own, new, future.

A COURT MARTIAL FOR LUNCH?

I returned to my duties in the mess hall, 50th Engineer Company, West Point, NY. One of the benefits of being in New York at that time is that the drinking age was 18 years old. I was legal! I didn't have to wait till I was 21 to drink. I could legally do it now! And, so I did.

New Year's Eve came soon after Christmas, as it often does. My leave had been cut short, so not to waste what was left of my leave time, I returned to duty as soon as I returned to the Point, just two days after Christmas. I was put on the duty roster as assistant cook with the junior cook in the food service section in charge. I think his name was Kenny, but that may not be correct. We were scheduled to work in the mess hall New Year's Day.

We had partied pretty much all night, and we really were not sober when we got to the mess hall at 4:30 AM to prepare breakfast for the 15 or 20 people still there over the holidays. We managed breakfast without too much effort, because everyone else was also still drunk, and nobody wanted much more that coffee, and maybe a piece of toast.

We finished breakfast, and had to immediately begin preparing for lunch, which was on the menu as beef stew. We had to cut up the beef, have a drink, cut up the vegetables, have a drink, find the appropriate pots and pans, have a drink. You get the picture. It was, after all, New Year's Day, a holiday, and we really didn't think anyone would notice. We weren't falling down drunk, just had a really good buzz on, and a wee bit giggly.

The stew was ready, more in spite of than because of us, at about 11:30. Lunch wasn't until 12:00 noon, so we had another drink. And then we poured a fifth of Four Roses Whiskey into the stew. That made it much better, in our humble opinions. Lunch was going well, and then, there was some sort of commotion in the dining area.

145

"Attention", someone yelled. And here came General Knowlton, Commanding General of the United States Military Academy, West Point, New York, and Superintendent of the United States Military Academy. This is the historical West Point that Benedict Arnold notoriously and traitorously surrendered to the British during the American War for Independence. The General is going to share lunch with the common enlisted soldiers.

What's for lunch? Beef Stew... made with the finest (or perhaps it was the cheapest) whiskey available. We're dead. Court-martialed. Keel Hauled. Hung from the yardarm. 40 lashes at high noon. Nope, he liked the stew so much that he asked for seconds.

There is nothing like the relief of seeing a senior officer leave your work area, pleased with your work, and having the knowledge that you are NOT going to jail. However, we did notice that the entire series of events was a tremendous buzz-kill. We were going to have to start drinking all over again, just to celebrate not getting caught drinking on duty. Anyway, I think we survived.

I kept in touch with Phyllis, of course, as we were falling in love. She decided to come up to visit in mid February 1972. I booked her a room in one of the local motels, and awaited her arrival. She drove up from DC in her Mercury and made pretty good time.

I took her on a tour of the Academy and the surrounding countryside. We spent a good part of one afternoon exploring West Point's Cemetery. There were gravestones dating back to the 1700's. The Cemetery has many a tale to tell. Simply reading the names and dates gives one pause to reflect on the consequences of historical decisions and actions, and on the ideals of Duty, Honor, Country as taught at the Academy.

We looked at the school buildings, the black powder cannon aimed down the Hudson River, the Military Academy Chapel. We enjoyed meals in the commissary as well as in the restaurants and sandwich shops in the adjacent town of Highland Falls.

There was the most wonderful Deli just outside the gates of the Point. I have yet to find a better pastrami on rye sandwich, anywhere. Their pickles were the shape and the size of the World War II Japanese miniature submarines. But they tasted way, way better than a Japanese submarine would. I seem to remember several meals there that week. The food was not only delicious, it was also inexpensive.

We took a drive on Monday night, February 14, simply enjoying the Milky Way's myriad stars in the black skies of a new moon. We drove a mountain road circling around the backside of West Point, driving past the ski slopes. There were Cadets, night skiing on the slopes, carrying torches, creating a beautiful, greeting card scene.

We parked on a scenic overlook. I took an engagement ring out of my pocket and asked Phyllis to marry me. She didn't immediately say "Yes", but she also didn't say "No", and she did agree to wear the ring. At least long enough to see if she could get used to the idea.

Yes, I proposed on Valentine's Day. I guess I am just a hopeless romantic. The rest of the week was simply time spent together. Unfortunately, the week passed very quickly, and Phyllis had to return to Ft. Belvoir.

Life took an unexpected and unforeseen turn very soon thereafter. With the war in Viet Nam winding down, President Nixon offered an early release for military members who were within 6 months of their normal discharge date, and Phyllis met this criteria. Early release was offered, and she accepted. She was given an Honorable Discharge from the United States Army on March 17, 1972, Saint Patrick's Day.

Upon her release, she packed her car and drove to West Point. She found an apartment with a roommate, an airline stewardess in a relationship with an officer stationed at West Point.

We enjoyed our time together, getting to know one another. Phyllis got a job at the Post Exchange, and I continued in my role as the Mess Clerk. And, then, things changed again, as they are wont to do. I was given orders re-assigning me to Fort Leonard Wood, Missouri. I gathered my few belongings and got ready for the transfer. Phyllis prepared to return to her home in Minnesota, intending to continue her education in Detroit Lakes, Minnesota.

Shortly after I left for Fort Leonard Wood, she packed up and began her long drive home to Hoffman, Minnesota. She arrived home, visited with family and friends for a couple months, and then continued north to Detroit Lakes, where she enrolled in the Fashion Merchandising program at the Detroit Lake Vocational/Technical School.

FORT LEONARD WOOD

Once again, we were separated, but not apart. I was in Ft. Leonard Wood and Phyllis was in Minnesota. We called and wrote letters. We exchanged cards, gifts and dreams of a future life together.

I managed to get to Minnesota to see Phyllis a few times. On one of my journeys to Minnesota, another soldier in my unit was driving to his home in Sioux City, Iowa, and invited me along for the ride. It would get me that much closer, and I could then take the bus straight up the Western edge of Minnesota to Hoffman, Phyllis' home town. It was eight hours in a car with several other bodies, and another 10 hours on Greyhound. I was tired when I finally arrived, but seeing her was well worth the discomfort.

We visited and she introduced me to her folks. I met her Mom and Oscar. I met her Mother and Father, as well as her sister and her husband and a multitude of Aunts, Uncles and cousins. Her Mom was actually her Aunt Irene, her Father's sister. Oscar was Irene's husband, and they had raised Phyllis and her sister, Gloria.

Phyllis' Father, Walter had been married to Eldonna. Walter thought Eldonna was going to divorce him, so he filed to divorce her. Regardless, they divorced when Phyllis was very young, and she had been raised by Irene and Oscar.

While I was there, the plan was for me to stay at the lake cabin, and Phyllis would stay in her folk's home in Hoffman. She and I watched television and visited late into the evening, when we fell asleep. We didn't awaken until the following morning. Irene was aghast that we had spent the night together.

Phyllis' car had been parked there at the cabin all night. Everyone in town knew that Phyllis had a fellow visiting from somewhere else, but what would the neighbors think now?! They would obviously think that she was immoral, a loose woman! We were so very innocent, and so clearly guilty. Thank goodness my visit was to be a short one. Meeting the parents is never as easy as one thinks it should be. They are, after all, just people.

I was relieved to be returning to Ft. Leonard Wood. My job at Leonard Wood was the operation of the tool room. Each mechanic had his own toolbox, but they occasionally needed other, more exotic, specialty tools. I maintained inventory control over these specialty tools, signing them out to mechanics when they had need of them, and then signed them back in when the job was completed. Boring. Boring! BORING!!!

While at Leonard Wood, I took leave to return to my Southern California home. Trust me, I was in need of respite from the Army, from the Ozarks, from those people in Missouri who believe that education beyond the 6th grade is just a waste of time. Not everyone I met in Missouri was like that, but the few that were, were dumb enough for the entire state's educational average to drop by several statistically relevant points.

However, as a simple point of fact, these people can be found just about anywhere. For some reason, the ones I met in Missouri were colorful enough and interesting enough, in their own bizarre way, to make an imprint in my memory.

But, then again, I have done some things that were not so very bright. Case in point: My plan was to fly home to California, and then drive back to Missouri in my Peugeot. However, my Peugeot needed a water pump. And, as a reminder, I am a trained mechanic in the United States Army. I pissed away my money hanging out with, and partying with, friends. I did not replace the water pump.

I still thought I'd be OK, just take it easy on the drive. I can take the Interstate pretty much all the way there. Except a friend of a friend or a sister's friend or a brother's friend... somebody needed a ride South, and they said it didn't really matter which way I went. So, I gave him a ride. Now, however, I was closer to I-10 than I was to I-15. I-15 would take me through the Rockies, Nevada, Utah, Colorado and so on. I-10 was the route through the desert.

On my second day out, somewhere in the Arizona desert, my water pump gave out. That shouldn't surprise anyone, not even me. I sat in my car by the side of the road in temperatures somewhere above 100 degrees. I had brought 5-gallon containers of water, so I soaked towels and put them over the windows, trying to capture any breeze that might wander by.

I sat there for several hours, through the hottest part of the day. I became dehydrated and began hallucinating, talking to people who weren't really there. And singing... loudly. That, in and of itself, was sufficient cause to be concerned. There were periods of lucidity when I knew that I was in trouble. An Arizona State Trooper finally stopped at about sunset. He radioed for a tow truck and the tow truck took me to the nearest small town. I'm still not real sure where I was, just somewhere in the Arizona desert.

The car was towed to a garage, and I checked into a motel for the night. I drank all the water I could, and spent a long time in a cool shower. I got up the next morning and went to the garage. They told me they could get a water pump, but it would take a week. In addition, I still owed payment for the tow into the shop. And, I still had to get back to Ft. Leonard Wood, or I will be AWOL!

I ended up selling my tools and the car, as well as anything and everything else they were willing to pay for. I didn't get a lot of money, but enough to make another bad decision. OK, maybe not a bad decision, as such, just that there were better decisions to be made.

I caught a bus to Phoenix, and then a flight, not to Missouri, but to Minnesota to see Phyllis for a couple of days. The better option would have been to report back to base, and save the leave for another time less fraught with troubles. Anyway, I visited Phyllis for a few simply glorious days before continuing on to Leonard Wood. There were a number of valuable lessons learned. And, it seems that everyone has some lessons that they have to learn on their own. These lessons are often learned with a certain amount of pain. But regardless, I was back. It was same stuff, different day.

The good news was that there were at Fort Leonard Wood, other, official activities that we could pursue on a semi-voluntary basis. One of the best entertainments available was being assigned to Aggressor Detail. Ft Leonard Wood was, at that time, also a Basic Training Facility. The recruits had been training for several weeks, and were taken out on bivouac. Bivouac is sort of a camping trip, Army style. Our job was to make one night of that camping trip a living hell for the recruits.

We began our mission early. This simply means we started drinking cheap wine and smoking pot at about midnight. Both were against regulations. By the time we were to carry out our "mission", we weren't drunk or stoned, but we did have a pretty good buzz going.

Our instructions were to "use any and every means available to attack the bivouac at approximately 0200 hours, utilizing smoke grenades, artillery simulator, blank ammunition in M-16 rifles and M-60 machine guns and any other smoke and/or noise generating devices that might be available. Booby trap escape routes with trip wire activated smoke and concussion devices. String rope and/or trip wire between and among the tents. Create as much disorientation and disruption as possible in a 30 minute window of opportunity. Capture as many sentries as possible without detection prior to the commencement of the aforementioned exercise." We also had extremely loud, military grade, whistling pyrotechnics to add to the chaos.

In other words, we were to violently disrupt the sleep of several hundred young men and scare the hell out of them. I've never had so much fun in my life. I'm not sure who thought of capturing black snakes and throwing them into random pup tents where guys were sleeping, but it was kind of a nice touch. Tying the sentries to trees in their underwear with their shirts over their heads might have been a bit much, but we figured they would either get themselves loose, or would be found by their units when the sun came up.

When the exercise was initiated, the chaos was complete. Guys were running everywhere, tripping over our obstacles and trip wires. Flash/bangs were going off, creating a surrealistic, strobe lit scene of violence, confusion and destruction.

Every time recruits ran, we headed them off and herded them into a classic ambush of sustained automatic weapons fire and grenade simulators. There was yelling and cursing, orders and counter orders being screamed back and forth. A few soldiers kept their heads and tried to assess the situation, but they were indeed, few.

We finally withdrew and returned to our Company area, drinking and smoking cigarettes and pot all the way back. We laughed and congratulated each other for our creativity and dedication in carrying out our orders. We were reasonably sure that our actions that night had not made us any friends. We rather hoped that they would not find out that it had been our unit tasked that night with aggressor detail. There was way too much potential for those enterprising young soldiers to return the "favor", if they ever discovered who had attacked them.

Should I feel bad about this exercise? I don't think so. I went through it, and every other recruit in the US Army, or any of the other services, has gone through something very similar. It really is one of those nights in Basic Training that you never forget, and I would never deprive them of that experience. It is right up there with the tear gas chamber.

It was soon after this event that I began developing a problem in my left arm. I started losing strength in my left arm, and my arm, from the shoulder down, ached, almost constantly. The doctors at Ft Leonard Wood were perplexed, so I was transferred to Fitzsimmons Army Medical Center in Denver CO.

I spent the next six weeks undergoing a variety of physical and neurological exams and procedures. One of these procedures involved placing electrodes in my shoulder and in my hand, inducing current, and then measuring that current to ascertain the connectivity and conductivity of my nervous system. It was not what I consider "fun".

After several weeks they said I no longer had a problem, and I could return to duty. I reported to an office wherein reigned a woman that could not, by any measure, be considered attractive. However, I had been made aware that it was she who would determine where my next duty station was to be. I was sufficiently forewarned to tread lightly.

What was my plan? I smiled. I was nice, I was respectful, and I called her 'Miss'. There was a sharp edge to her, and she was somewhat abrasive, so, I was nice. I smiled. I may even have playfully flirted. I told a couple of jokes, just throw away lines I always have with me. It took a couple of trips to the office on different days, but I stayed nice, kept talking and kept smiling.

Then I asked her where I might be assigned. I had about a year and a half remaining on my enlistment, so this new assignment would probably be my last duty station. With over a year to go, I wanted someplace that was not going to be too difficult.

She mentioned a couple of duty locations that I was just not interested in. I did not want to go to Fort Polk in Louisiana. I did not want to go to Korea. I did not want to go to Alaska. I certainly did not want to go to Viet Nam!

Then she asked, "How would you like to go to the Presidio of San Francisco?" I had no idea what the Presidio of San Francisco was, but as I remembered from school, San Francisco is in California. I was a California native. Yes, I was most interested in this assignment, but was she capable of making this happen? Yes? Yes, not only was she able to do this, she did do this. She got me transferred to D Company, 864th Engineer Battalion, Presidio of San Francisco for my final year and a few months in the US Army. SCORE!

Actually, she was nice. She was simply used to having to be overly assertive to the point of abrasiveness, simply to be taken seriously. The Army had stifled yet another human being. Her primary motivation was the fear that someone would take an interest in her, and, even if it were a casual friendship, she would have no idea how to interact with another human being. And, she was much less unattractive when she actually smiled.

I flew home to Southern California for a one-week leave, and then flew to San Francisco. San Francisco Airport is actually in South San Francisco, and requires a bus ride to downtown, another bus ride to the Presidio, and then a base cab to the new duty station, Company D, 864th Engineer Battalion, Presidio of San Francisco, detached from 9th Infantry Division, Fort Lewis, Washington.

A new chapter opens. I am now 21 years old, engaged to the girl of my dreams and living in San Francisco, a time and a place ripe with promise and potential.

PRESIDIO OF SAN FRANCISCO

Company D, 864th Engineers, Presidio of San Francisco. Our barracks were old, two story mission style buildings of stucco with red tile roofs. The upper floor had been divided into rooms on both sides of a long central hallway, each room set up for 4 men.

Each man's contained a military bunk, a footlocker and a wall locker. We arranged wall lockers to divide the room in half, with 2 men to each half. It was somehow better having only one roommate as opposed to having 3 roommates. Yes, I know, we were all still in the same room, but we created an illusion of 2 separate rooms. The community bathrooms and showers were just down the hall.

In this environment, there were social divisions among the soldiers stationed there. One such military distinction was based on where we had each been stationed, whether or not the soldier had been to Viet Nam. Other social differentiations were made between those who drank alcohol, and those who chose to smoke marijuana.

Keep in mind that this is happening in San Francisco, at one time the epicenter of the anti Viet Nam War movement. The Presidio was just across the Bay from Berkley, home of People's Park and the Free Speech Movement. UC Berkley was known as one of the birthplaces of the entire College/University Anti-war Movement.

The year was 1973. Flower Power was still, in many ways, actually in power! The world was colorful and psychedelic and the music was everywhere. Peace and LOVE, my brothers and sisters, Peace and Love!

I made friends with the guys I was stationed with. This is normal. Tim was from Montana, with dreams of becoming an attorney. There was Pete, from Carson City, Nevada, a good mechanic who had served a tour in South Viet Nam. He managed to make it home over the high Sierras to Nevada at least once a month. He later became an accountant, working in and for the State of Nevada. There was yet another Pete, this one from Minnesota.

There was Grant, from Northern California, near Garberville. He knew where to buy the best marijuana in California's Emerald Triangle, and, he knew the people. If you didn't know the people, you didn't get the pot. It really was just that simple. Grant's Dad was a Sergeant with the California Highway Patrol.

Guenther was from Ohio, a place he never wanted to return to. His Uncle Bill was a bit older than were we, had a very cool apartment in San Francisco, worked for the US Post Office, and a beautiful wife named Linda, whom he treated like crap.

Oh, and we cannot forget Killer Kelly! I'm not sure if Kelly was even 5' tall. And, for a short fellow, he sure carried around enough stupid for several guys. He had a personality--if you can even call it that--that not even his mother could possibly love. His uniform was always starched, creased, perfect . . . until you got to his face. His face and his head was as perfectly round as any human face I have ever seen. And his face was covered with what was possibly the single worst case of acne ever recorded.

If Kelly was there, something was going to go wrong, something was going to break. If you gave him a ride in your car, you would get a flat tire, or a rock would hit your windshield. You didn't want him anywhere near if you were working on a piece of equipment, especially if you had to get under it. If he was there, it would fall on you. If he walked past a goldfish pond, the fish would drown. That was Killer Kelly.

I suppose we should be ashamed, as we were fairly abusive of Kelly. He seemed to accept the abuse as a better option than being ignored completely. There were times when one guy would distract him just before the Company was called to attention. Other GIs would put their still lit cigarettes in his pockets. While the rest of us were standing at rigid attention, he would be jumping and dancing around, beating his pockets, trying to put the cigarettes out. There was smoke coming from his pockets, and we all thought it was so funny. I'm truly sorry, Kelly, it really wasn't funny, and it isn't funny, picking on someone lacking the ability to fight back.

We stood formation every morning in front of the barracks, and then drove down to the motor pool, either in our own cars or in an Army van. The motor pool was right on the water of San Francisco Bay. If you stood looking at the bay with the motor pool behind you, you could see Alcatraz in the middle of the bay. Directly to the right was the Coast Guard Station.

Across the bay, was Marin County with tree-covered hills rising up from the Bay. To the left was the Golden Gate Bridge and Fort Point, a Civil War era fort built to guard the entrance to San Francisco against hostile, Rebel naval forces that might try to sail through the Golden Gate.

In the early 1970s, the conflict in Viet Nam was still raging, and American soldiers were still dying on a daily basis. We were honored to be asked to provide the Honor Guard and Funeral Detail for military funerals conducted in the area. We trained diligently and wore our best, dress green uniforms and chromed helmets, with white ceremonial, Sam Browne style web gear.

We escorted the casket to the cemetery, served as pallbearers, and stood Honor Guard at the head and foot of the casket. During internment, our seven-man squad fired three spaced volleys from our M16s for the 21-gun salute. Our bugler played Taps from a nearby hillside, its mournful notes carried on the afternoon breeze.

We were privileged to present these final honors to those who had given their last full measure of devotion to their country, to our country. I must admit, that at times, it was incredibly difficult to maintain the required stoicism in the presence of so much emotion, so much sorrow. We did so, however, with pride, honor and respect. We were duty bound to honor our brothers in arms, and, in so doing, to provide some small measure of comfort to the family of the deceased.

One such funeral stands out. As I said, we stood our posts at the casket in rigid parade rest. There was a formal change of the guard every half hour. The detail Sergeant would slow march the relief guards to casket, bring the current guards to attention, salute the casket, relieve and replace the guard, and withdraw. It was all done in "slow time", each movement, the march, the salute, the withdrawal, precise.

I was standing at the head of a casket, and could overhear the conversation among the funeral attendees as they reminisced about the young soldier being laid to rest. The conversation turned to the military formality of the funeral, and of our participation. They began asking among themselves how we, the Honor Guard, could stand so still, so rigid for so long.

I'm still not sure why, but for some reason, their focus on us, not on the deceased, bothered me. It angered me. They were talking of us as though we were just another piece of the furnishings. Their focus should have been on the deceased, not on us. We were there to honor their fallen soldier, to show respect for his service, his sacrifice. Why could they not do the same?

Invariably, the return trip to the Presidio was always very quiet, very reflective.

At one point in early 1973, before Phyllis arrived in San Francisco, Grant and I thought it would be a good idea to drive to Southern California, hook up with a friend of my sister's and buy a quantity of LSD. We could buy 100 hits of windowpane acid in Southern California for $75, and we could then sell them for $3 apiece in San Francisco. It seemed like a good idea at the time.

We climbed into Grant's Triumph GT+6, a closed cockpit, 2 seat, British sports car, and headed south. We made good time going down, and spent a couple of days visiting with family and friends. We made our illicit purchase, loaded up and headed north on I-5.

As soon as we crested the Grapevine, we each took a hit of the acid we had just bought. This was NOT one of our better decisions. I-5 through central California is the longest, straightest, most boring road in the world especially after dark, which just happens to be when we were making the drive.

We pulled off the interstate somewhere in California's Central Valley to get gas. We didn't have much money left, but we got what we could. Grant had been "drifting" behind semi trucks, a technique in which you get very close to the large commercial vehicle in front of you and allow its slipstream to pull you along. Drifting can actually increase your mileage by a substantial factor. However, I do not recommend this. It can be very dangerous, especially when you have taken LSD, your senses are totally distorted and you are hallucinating.

While we were at the gas station, a guy on a chopped and customized Harley pulled in. Even after he had gotten off of his motorcycle, he continued to vibrate and shake. Obviously a case of rigid frame shakes. We felt sorry for him, so gave him 2 hits of acid, which he promptly popped into his mouth. We didn't know where he was headed, but we were pretty sure it was going to be an interesting ride.

We got back in the car and continued north on I-5. We were tripping pretty good by this time, but neither of us was smart enough to pull over and let it wear off. Oh, no, we had to keep going. Except for our hallucinations, the rest of the trip went fairly well; until we got to the Oakland Bay Bridge.

The fare to cross the bridge was $.50. We didn't have $.50. We had put everything into the gas tank, just to get this far. The toll taker told us he could accept a check, so I wrote a check for $.50. We made it back to the Presidio at about 3:00 in the morning. It was a good thing that we didn't have to stand morning formation until 6:30. We were still out of our minds, but no one seemed to notice. So much for our version of the Electric Acid, Kool-Aid test!

I had been at the Presidio for 3 or 4 months when Phyllis completed her Degree in Fashion Merchandising at Detroit Lakes Vocational/Technical School in Minnesota. We had remained in contact the entire time, writing cards and letters back and forth, and calling on the phone when we could afford it. The decision for her to come to San Francisco to had been jointly made.

For the first few days, we stayed in Tim and Lori's apartment, but this only lasted a few days. Tim and I were in the same platoon, and worked together pretty much every day. Sunday morning, we had all been reading different parts of the newspaper, and Tim went off. He began yelling about the mess, and began crumpling up the newspaper and shoving it in the trash. Phyllis and I decided we would rather be somewhere else, so we got up and left. We kept the classified ads from the paper and began looking for an apartment of our own.

We finally found a 3rd floor walk-up apartment on Cabrillo Street, a short block from Golden Gate Park, two or three blocks from Ocean Beach, and just a couple of miles from the Presidio. There was a bus stop on the corner where Phyllis could catch a bus to go to work downtown.

I was required to maintain a bunk and locker in the barracks, but there was no requirement for me to stay there when I was off duty. I could still eat a couple of meals in the mess hall every day for free, and my wall locker gave me a place to store my military gear.

Our apartment was in a block of similar apartments, all of a uniform size and shape, with narrow access spaces and narrow alleys between buildings. Other apartment blocks seemed to have agreed on different heights, with some of 3 floors, some with 4, and a few in the distance, of 5 and 6 stories. Our building had a parking garage on the ground floor, so, although we were on the third story, we were on the Second Floor, and there was one apartment above us.

The apartment has a living room, a bedroom, a kitchen and bath. There is a back door in the kitchen that opens onto a small landing. From the landing, stairs ascended from the ground floor, past our apartment and up the stairs up to the flat roof. The stairwell wound back and forth, providing access to two floors and eight doors in four separate apartment buildings. I don't remember ever seeing anyone else making use of it. Oh wait, there was that one time...

Phyllis and I were in the kitchen, and the back door was open to capture a small breath of ocean breeze. We heard a loud commotion that sounded like it was coming from our roof! What the heck is going on? Phyllis and I quickly started up the stairs.

We had just barely gotten our heads above the top of the stairway when we saw a police officer running across an adjacent roof, chasing a suspect, and carrying his service weapon two-handed at high ready. Each of them, cop and suspect, each in turn, jumped over the 5 foot gap between that building and ours and ran across our roof, right past us!

As he ran across our roof, the Policeman yelled at us to get back inside and lock the door! We ran back down the stairs, into our apartment, and yes, we locked the door. We then heard sirens converging on our location. It was easy to track them from the sounds of the siren.

First, they went toward the ocean, then turned north. Next they doubled back to the south, toward Golden Gate Park. We figured that this was probably not be a good time to go outside. So, we did not. We stayed inside for the better part of the next several hours. We stayed put, listened to records and smoked pot. That seemed to us to be the best plan.

Throughout the day, we would overhear police radios in the patrol cars swarming our quiet little street. We never did find out what the whole thing was about. Just one of those San Francisco things, I guess.

Phyllis found a job with an advertising agency in downtown San Francisco. She rode the bus to work most days, as it really was the most efficient way of getting around. I drove a little Opal Kadette station wagon. It had a wimpy motor and a four speed, manual transmission. This was not the best car for San Francisco's steep hills.

Downhill wasn't bad, but uphill could be a challenge. I learned to use the emergency brake to give me time to get my foot off of the brake and on to the gas pedal. Give it some gas, release the clutch and slowly release the hand brake. No problem, senor. Fortunately, the road to and from Presidio wasn't too bad.

Phyllis' office was retained by the movie distribution companies to advertising new movies just being released. The people she worked with were all artistic, creative, funky, and just a little off center. Her co-workers were true San Franciscans, liberal and tolerant of anything and everything.

They went to Renaissance Fairs, wore the garb and participated in the activities. One couple even went so far as to be married at the Faire, and in costume. 'Twas very... enchanting, I guess would be the word.

A majority of her male co-workers were gay. It was, even then, San Francisco. I was comfortable enough in my own, male, heterosexuality that that was never an issue. I wasn't concerned about it. This is simply a point of observation pertinent to the next part of my story.

During the course of the year, the company would observe holidays and celebrations by having parties in their large conference room, adjacent to the in-house movie theatre. This is where staff watched new release movies to know how best to advertise the new movies, nationwide. I should also mention that their snack bar served beer, wine and mixed drinks, as well as snacks...at no charge. This made for a pretty inexpensive night out.

We were invited to one such seasonal party (I can't remember which one) and we were enjoying the festivities. After the welcoming speeches, everyone began to drink and mingle. A few minutes later, there was an announcement that the movie was going to begin. We weren't sure which movie would be screened, but anticipated some newly released production. And, sure enough, that was what we got.

I don't remember the movie itself, but I will certainly never forget the way in which it was shown; a reel of movie, a reel of hardcore porn, a reel of the movie, a reel of porn. This is where the gay part becomes significant to the story. The porn was all heterosexual porn, but it was the gay guys that watched the porn with the greatest intensity! Most of the rest of us simply patronized the bar, mingled and socialized.

I really preferred the weekly screenings on Wednesdays when employees were allowed to invite a guest to the screening of new, soon to be released movies. Movies had to be screened for advertising purposes, so it was a perk for the employees to invite a guest to watch these brand new movies. We saw Bruce Lee in Enter the Dragon, American Graffiti and The Sting. And we got to see them before they were released to theatres.

As I said, our apartment was only a block from Golden Gate Park, and, quite naturally, we spent a good part of our time in the park. On one such occasion, we encountered a large crowd of colorful San Francisco denizens, and they all appeared to be waiting for something to happen.

That something turned out to be a live music recording. Staff walked through the crowd, handing out the lyrics to a song called "Sons of 1984", to be recorded by Todd Rungren and with our participation.

He had previously recorded the same song, again with audience participation, in Central Park, New York City. It was his plan to combine the two sessions for a "coast to coast" recording of the song. Phyllis and I had no place we had to be, nothing we had to do, so we stuck around, adding our voices to all of the others. We "performed" it several times, with the record producers and sound engineers striving for that perfect sound. And, yes, the song is still available on line.

We took drives across the Golden Gate Bridge to Marin County, where there were a couple of side-by-side nightclubs sharing both a parking lot and customers, Zack's and The Boathouse. People could, and would, simply wander from one to the other.

On Saturdays, you wanted to arrive early for the turtle races. "OK, what? Turtle races?" you might ask. The bar had a number of turtles in their stable, each with a number painted on its shell. They would pick 5 turtles at random and put them under a washtub in the middle of a large circle painted on the floor and roped off.

When the washtub was lifted, the first turtle to pass the outer circle was deemed the winner. Some would move quickly, and some would just stay where they were. There was no way to tell the difference. You couldn't gamble for real money, but you could win drinks, shirts, meals and more. It was usually fun, always loud, a little bit crazy, and the drinks were cheap.

We would often take others from our respective work places with us. Funny, it now occurs to me that it was always Phyllis' liberal, San Francisco friends, or my friends from the military, one or the other, very seldom both at the same time. How curious!

A favorite destination was arrived at over a dirt track in the mountains facing the sea north of San Francisco. There exist World War II artillery and spotter instillations carved into the mountains, and we enjoyed exploring them. There were, and probably still are, concrete tunnels crisscrossing through the mountain. These are spotter's perches where men would scan the skies with binoculars, watching for planes from the west, those bearing the rising sun of the Japanese fleet.

Although still illegal at every level of government, it was during this period in San Francisco that we began using marijuana on a more or less regular basis. The majority of our friends, both military and civilian were smoking. It had become almost commonplace and, in many arenas, socially acceptable.

We went to a "Great American Smoke-Out" at the Berkley City Hall. Somewhere around 2,000 to 2,500 people dressed up, showed up, and lit up. There really were way too many people smoking pot for the police to be able to take any effective action. That, in and of itself, was a significant part of the plan. There were people carrying grocery sacks full of pre-rolled joints that they simply threw indiscriminately into the crowd! A massive blue cloud of cannabis smoke encircled City Hall, and there really was nothing the authorities could do about it!

The only bizarre event in this whole episode, as if the entire event wasn't bizarre enough in its own right, is when a couple of women grabbed a random guy and started trying to take off his jeans. They were acting in an excessively sexual manner, almost as if they were performing a scripted, dramatic role in theatre.

It was later discovered and revealed that these two women were indeed, undercover surrogates for the police. They were presenting their best performance to cast the entire event in a negative, Reefer Madness, kind of light. When the instigators couldn't get the pot smokers to do anything outrageous, they took it upon themselves to add a little "local color". It turned out that they were prostitutes, and, if they did as requested by the police, their charges would be reduced or dropped. They failed miserably.

There were a lot of other drugs available in and around the San Francisco bay at that time. It was easy to find LSD, cocaine, opium, hash and other substances. Other than marijuana and hashish, we stayed away from most of the other drugs, although we did experiment a few times with LSD.

Our first acid trip was at Guenther's Uncle Bill's apartment. Bill began playing Pink Floyd's Dark Side of The Moon album, a record I had never before heard. When the alarms in the song "Time" went off, I was on acid and incredibly startled by the alarm bells.

I jumped up from my seat on the end of the couch and accidently knocked down a hanging plant. Emmet was sitting on a cushion on the floor next to me, and the falling plant fell on his head, covering his head in a cascade of dirt and plant material. He, too, was on acid, and having a plant fall on his head did nothing to improve the experience.

Our ride over to the party had already been rough on Emmet. He had taken acid before we picked him up at the barracks, and he was already beginning to feel the effects. I was driving my Opal Kadette, with Emmet in the back seat, and Phyllis in the passenger seat next to me. Our route took us up and down and over hills, through multiple turns in the traffic route. At one such turn, there were 3 left turn lanes, and we were in the center turn lane between two city transit busses. Emmet's perception was already compromised, so the movement in that small car as it kept pace with the two busses through the left turn was difficult for him to contend with.

Their apartment was a typical hippy pad, although nicer than most. Bill was a mail carrier and made good money, so they bought nicer things for their home, just in that psychedelic, hippy style. There were beanbag chairs and large cushions spread everywhere, no couch, but did have a large, very comfortable, overstuffed chair in the living room. There were black lights and black light posters, strobe lights and a tremendous sound system, with four-foot tall tower speakers, loud enough to cause serious brain damage.

We partied like it was 1973! We went to concerts at Winter Land, and saw J Geils, Sha Na Na, and a Dutch group named Focus performed a very strange yodeled piece of music called "Hocus Pocus". We attended more shows and more acts than I can remember, averaging better than 2 performances a month. There are reasons I can no longer remember the names of all of the groups we saw. Re read the first sentence of this paragraph. "We partied like it was 1973." Oh, yeah, it was 1973!

Curiously, we attended the Sha Na Na concert when Tony came up to San Francisco to share our first Thanksgiving together, Phyllis and I. The opening act for Sha Na Na was the Electric Light Orchestra! At that time, Sha Na Na was the bigger act, and ELO was just coming into its own.

We got through our year in San Francisco with the help of our friends. Phyllis had Pat English, whose last name was not English, but she was indeed, British. This ploy helped to differentiate Pat English from the other Pat. I suppose we could have just used her given last name, but I don't know that I ever heard it.

I had made friends with the men I was stationed with, of course; Grant, AJ, Guenther, the other two Pete's. While stationed at the Presidio, I took advantage of the Army Education Center, and completed the California requirements for a high school diploma. I had attended high school in California, and already had my GED, but I wanted that high school diploma. As I recall, I only needed three classes; an English class, Political Science and an elective.

This was one of those rare times where everything came together as it should. We all liked each other, everyone got along. Although it was one of the most diverse groups I had ever been associated with, we had no dissenters or disrupters. We were male and female, white, black, Hispanic, Japanese and Samoan.

There was also one older, misplaced Frenchman, recently of the French Foreign Legion, now in the service of the Army of the United States of America. His ultimate goal was to become an American citizen, and one way to achieve that goal was by serving in the military.

Mr. Thomas was the Political Science Instructor, and Roz taught English and Biology. Several of the students, Roz and I as well as some of the other instructors began socializing after hours. We had the Biology classes at the education center in the evening, and when the class ended, we would sometimes go out to get something to eat. Occasionally, on weekends, we would go out as a group for drinks, and sometimes, dancing. There was no hanky-panky involved. We were just co-workers and friend that liked to hang out together.

Roz asked for volunteers to help her move. She was living in Sausalito and drove across the Golden Gate Bridge every day. She really wanted to move into San Francisco. The new apartment was closer to work, she would spend less on gas, and there was a perception of a greater opportunity for a more active social life in the city.

So, several of us did offer to help her move into what turned out to be a much smaller San Francisco apartment, where, to her dismay, I expressed my opinion of her move. She was getting "... half the place for twice the price". She was not amused. It was too close to the truth to be funny.

I ran into Roz again in Denver several years later, but the rest of that story is for a later chapter.

San Francisco was a fascinating interlude in the adventure that was my life. About 6 months prior to my military discharge, I was allowed to go into "Project Transition". This was a program in which the Army allowed soldiers to spend the working day in civilian positions in an attempt to ease our return to civilian life. Tim, also, was a part of the program. He went to work for an attorney, working as an intern/legal clerk.

Based on Aptitude/Interest Tests administered by the Army, I was assigned to a high school, working with the Boys' Counselor, and dealing with kids that may have had family, social or even criminal issues to be dealt with in the school environment. Much to my chagrin, the counselor to whom I was assigned was resentful of my presence. He felt as if I had been pawned off on him, with no benefit to him or his to his program.

The one case in which I expressed an opinion was enough for him to tell me not to come back. The case involved a young student who had been caught with marijuana. I said I hoped the next step would be education, not necessarily punishment. My input was promptly dismissed, and the kid was put through the wringer. They had no desire to help the kid. They simply wanted to use him as an example of the consequences of getting caught with pot. The only thing this accomplished was to teach the kids to be more cautious and sneakier.

I pretty much stopped going to the school, except to sign in and leave. They never seemed to miss me, and continued submitting reports to the Army that I was an exceptional asset, that they were fortunate to have me, blah, blah, blah. I took advantage of the time to get stoned on pot and continue exploring San Francisco.

There were a number of stories from San Francisco that have taken on a life of their own. Thanksgiving 1973, my younger brother, Tony came to visit and to share our turkey, along with several GIs from the Presidio. He stayed with us for most of a week, and we enjoyed his company. We took him on the cable cars all over San Francisco, to Fisherman's Wharf, Coit Tower and Ghirardelli Square.

Christmas of 1973, Phyllis and I had decided against buying a Christmas tree, opting instead to save our money by creating a tree out of gold wrapping paper, and taping it to the wall. Late on Christmas Day evening, near 11:00 pm, Grant and Guenther showed up at our apartment with a Christmas tree that they had stolen from a closed Christmas tree lot. Thanks a lot, guys. Something about a day late and a dollar short?

Several of the events recorded here actually occurred before Phyllis arrived in San Francisco, but they are remembered in the order presented here. I suppose I could go back and cut and paste the paragraphs, but right now, I'm trying to get as much of the story out as I can. If I remember where I left off, I may go back later and move them around. Then again, I might not. As I said earlier, I'm trying to give a flavor to the times, not a straight line, chronological history. All this happened in San Francisco. There may well be several really good reasons why I can't remember the order in which these events happened!

Later on that autumn, Phyllis and I decided to have a Halloween party. We invited our friends, both civilian and military. We invited Roz and Mr. Thomas, and everyone else we could think of. Hell, we even invited Killer Kelly! In preparation for the party, we took most of the furniture out of the living room, and picked up the large area rug. We left the table with the food and drinks, and the small throw rug under the rocking chair. We left one small rug, just one! Care to guess where Kelly puked when he had had too much to drink? Yep, on the small throw rug. The floor we could wash, but we never could get the smell out of the rug, so ended up having to throw it away.

I wore a Cavalry uniform; Phyllis was a Greek or Roman princess. Pete H came as a clown, and Roz showed up as a Catholic nun. She said that on her way to the party, she had cut off another car. That driver of that other car honked his horn and was prepared to be very angry with her. When he pulled even with her, he saw her in her nun's habit. She smiled and waved at him. He responded with his own wave and a, sheepish, slightly strained, smile. We had a good party.

When my enlistment ended in February 1974, I went home to Southern California to visit family, and to look for a place to live. Phyllis was not yet ready to leave her job in San Francisco, and we were taking a pause, a break from one another.

We were each to reflect on our relationship, to decide if we were supposed to be together, to see if we even wanted to be together. Phyllis was going to stay in San Francisco, and I was being given the opportunity to revisit the home and the friends of my youth, to discover if I really wanted to be in a serious, committed relationship with the ultimate goal being marriage.

It really didn't take us very long at all to decide that we really did want to be together. Such was our karma, such was our destiny. We were soul mates, we were supposed to be together. It was simple, and it was obvious. However, it was going take a while for us to have all of our stuff in the same place.

When I returned to So Cal, Phyllis found a new apartment in San Francisco, closer to her work, just outside of Chinatown. As it later turned out, her apartment was right across the street from the radio station where the Symbionese Liberation Army, the SLA, was dropping off communiqués regarding the kidnapped newspaper heiress, Patricia Hearst.

It was the major news story at the time. Patty Hearst, a college student, had been kidnapped and was being held prisoner by the SLA; she had some involvement in the armed robbery of the Hibernia Bank. Her father had been forced by the SLA to buy and distribute some $4 million worth of food in poor neighborhoods of the Bay Area. This ended when violent food riots broke out at the distribution points. The SLA had been involved in bank robberies, murders, the Patty Hearst kidnapping, and finally, a major gun battle in Los Angeles.

Anyway, I got a little sidetracked there. We were talking about the end of my enlistment, and my return to So Cal. After a short while in So Cal, I came to the conclusion that I missed Phyllis, so I decided to fly up to San Francisco for a few days with her. I did so, and we enjoyed our brief visit. The time for me to again return to So Cal came all too soon.

She rode the city bus out to San Francisco Airport with me, just to keep me company, and to extend our time together by just a little. We said our goodbyes, I prepared to board my flight. Phyllis got back on the bus to downtown San Francisco.

She arrived at the downtown bus terminal and began the walk back to her apartment. For the first few blocks, other people from the bus had been walking in her direction, but they had all turned off, one by one, until she was walking alone. The sun had set a couple hours ago, and the fog had rolled in. Haloed streetlights cast pools of pale light against the coming night. Lonely foghorns called out to one another on the Bay.

A car with three men in it cruised slowly by, with the men all looking at her. They slowed the car to match her pace, rolled down the car window, and began calling to her. As her fear began to mount, a large red dog walked up and positioned himself between Phyllis and the car. He looked at the car and began to growl deep, deep in his throat. The men in the car made a couple more efforts to get a reaction, but that big red dog was not going to allow them to do her any harm. They drove off, looking for easier prey.

When within about a half block from her apartment, the red dog ran ahead and sat down in her doorway. She was stunned. She took a minute to pet him and praise him, telling him what a good dog he was. She knew she had a nice piece of steak from a restaurant meal we had shared and thought to get it for the dog as a reward.

She ran into her apartment and was back outside in less than 90 seconds. The dog was nowhere to be seen. It was then that Phyllis realized that God had sent an angel to see her safely home, and he had certainly done that. She went back into her apartment and said a prayer of thanks.

Soon thereafter I found a job in a convenience store and a studio apartment on Warner Avenue in Huntington Beach. The apartment complex had four swimming pools, two hot tubs and was right across the street from a supermarket. Phyllis quit her job in San Francisco and moved in with me in Huntington Beach. The year was 1974, and a new chapter in my life was about to begin.

Rick, Celia, Phyllis, and Pete – Westminster, CA circa 1973

AFTERWORD

I am writing this afterword on August 6, 2017, as the work is being completed. I fully realize that there remain a substantial number of unanswered questions in my account of my life.

In this missive, I have tried to adhere pretty much to the truth, but the potential exists that there may well be unintentional embellishments in some areas. I'm not even sure that I could tell which episodes, which chapters, which stories, may have been embellished. I made an attempt to keep things in the correct chronological order, but, you can rest assured that I screwed that up as well.

I have, with malice of forethought, taken some literary license in how the story is presented. I'm afraid that otherwise it would probably be pretty boring. The facts are there, the truth, and the story, hopefully intertwined in an entertaining manner.

I am also obliged to point out that some stories in this book are based on decisions I have made in my life, and some of those decisions have been pretty disastrous. I have made substantial errors in judgment, verging on stupidity, and many of the consequences of those decisions are still with me today.

There were times when I drank too much. There were times when I said the wrong thing to the wrong person, and usually in the wrong way. I smoked cannabis when it was illegal, and the potential consequences of that decision to use pot far outweighed any pleasure that may have been derived.

I swallowed a pill or a piece of blotter paper that someone told me contained LSD. It could have been anything. There really was not a lot of quality control in the manufacture of unlawful substances at that time in our history.

Perhaps I could have pursued a better understanding for the motivation to pursue that experience, that short term release from reality. I'm still not sure why I did some of the things I did, but on a more mature reflection, I certainly could have made better decisions in that regard. The world is actually pretty OK without that particular modification.

Hallucinogenic drugs were, at that time, and in some segments of society, seen as a way to open and use more of one's own mind. There were a number of competing philosophies, each trying to establish a place. Drug use was seen as a vehicle to a greater metaphysical understanding, and to achieving a greater understanding of these philosophies, a "one-ness" with the Universe.

The point of the preceding paragraphs being: I didn't need cannabis, I didn't need alcohol, and I didn't need LSD to understand anything. I ran the potential of serious and permanent brain damage. I was stupid. Don't do what I did.

I do hope that I have acquired some wisdom over the years, but I continue to make mistakes. These, too have had, and continue to have, repercussions.

Sometimes, when you open up a can of worms, you sell worms. Sometimes when you open up a can of worms, you go fishing. Sometimes, when you open up a can of worms, it's best to just spill them all out. They are good for the soil and make the flowers bloom. And, that, too, can be a good trade; a can of worms for a field of flowers.

The point of this is that I hope it helps to give a better insight as to who I am. In – as – much as this work is intended for my progeny, as well as for (hopefully) greater, more widespread distribution, it may even help you, my progeny, figure out who you are, and why you think something is funny.

I have been writing pretty much all of my life, and on a number of subjects. In some of these subjects, I am fairly knowledgeable, in some, I am extrapolating, and making educated guesses, and, in some subjects, I am basically full of s**t. You will just have to read it in its entirety and make up your own mind as to which is which.

It was my intent to at least keep the episodes in what could be called location chronological order. I was born in Sacramento, California in 1952. I thereafter lived in the following locations in this order: Sacramento CA, Long Beach CA and/or its environs, Rawlins WY - Midway City CA - Midway City CA - Rock Springs WY - Midway City CA - Westminster CA - Fort ORD CA – Fort Belvoir VA – West Point NY – Fort Leonard Wood MO – Denver CO (Brief medical stay) – Presidio of San Francisco CA – Huntington Beach CA – Fort Polk LA – Fort Lewis WA – Fort Riley KS – Costa Mesa CA – Denver CO – Limon CO – Genoa CO - Huntington OR – Portland OR – Tillamook OR – Salem OR – Davenport WA – Spokane WA – Las Vegas NV – Reno NV – Las Vegas NV – Mira Loma CA – Las Vegas NV – Spokane WA – San Bernardino CA – Spokane WA.

I may have the time line screwed up within the locations at the time that they actually occurred, but if I relate a story in the third "Midway City CA", then the sequence of events may have been A, B, C, but I tell the story as C, A, B, but it happened in that third "Midway City CA" time frame.

TIMELINE

1960   John F Kennedy, defeated Richard M. Nixon, sworn in as President

1960   Soviets shoot down US U2 spy plane piloted by Francis Gary Powers.

1961   Soviet Cosmonaut Yuri Gagarin becomes the first person in space.

1961   Bay of Pigs fiasco, Cuba

1961   Construction of the Berlin Wall

1961   President Kennedy begins the Peace Corps

1962   The Cuban Missile Crisis

1962   US Troop buildup in Viet Nam begins

1962   First Wal-Mart opens

1963   President Kennedy is assassinated in Texas

1964   Senate ratifies Nuclear Test Ban Treaty

1965   Watts Riots in Los Angeles – 34 dead, National Guard Called Out

1965   Northeast Blackout darkens East Coast of US and Eastern Canada

1966   Supreme Court rules on and establishes Miranda Rights

1967   Arab/Israeli Six Day War – Israel defeats Egypt, Syria and Jordan

1967   Thurgood Marshall confirmed as the first African American Supreme Court Justice

1968   Richard Nixon elected President

1968   Soviets invade and crush popular uprising in Czechoslovakia

1968   Anti-Viet Nam War protests across US

1969   Apollo 11 lands on the moon.

1969   Woodstock

Made in the USA
Columbia, SC
18 February 2025